THE MAN WHO NEVER WAS

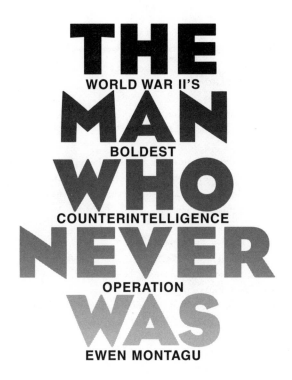

THE MAN WHO NEVER WAS

WORLD WAR II'S BOLDEST COUNTERINTELLIGENCE OPERATION

EWEN MONTAGU

BLUEJACKET BOOKS

Naval Institute Press
Annapolis, Maryland

Naval Institute Press
291 Wood Road
Annapolis, MD 21402

First Bluejacket Books printing, 2001

Library of Congress Cataloging-in-Publication Data
Montagu, Ewen, 1901–
    The man who never was : World War II's boldest counterintelligence operation / Ewen Montagu ; introduction by Alan Stripp.
        p.   cm.
    Originally published: New York : Oxford University Press, 1953.
    ISBN 1-55750-448-2
    1. Montagu, Ewen, 1901– 2. Operation Mincemeat. 3. World War, 1939–1945—Secret service—Great Britain. 4. World War, 1939–1945—Personal narratives, British. 5. World War, 1939–1945—Campaigns—Italy—Sicily.
D810.S8M6   2001
940.54'8641—dc21   00-052446

Printed in the United States of America on acid-free paper ♾
08 07 06 05 04 03   8 7 6 5 4 3 2

All photographs courtesy of the Public Record Office, WO 106/5921.

Contents

Foreword

TO MYSTIFY AND MISLEAD the enemy has always been one of the cardinal principles of war. Consequently, *ruses de guerre* of one kind or another have played a part in almost every campaign ever since the episode of the Trojan horse, or perhaps even earlier.

The game has been played for so long that it is not easy to think out new methods of disguising one's strength or one's intentions. Moreover, meticulous care must be exercised in the planning and execution of these schemes. Otherwise, so far from deceiving the enemy, they merely give the show away.

The Allies decided that their next step, after the battle for Tunisia, should be the invasion of Italy through Sicily. We felt sure—one always does on these occasions—that this was such an obvious corollary to the North African campaign, that the enemy would expect it and concentrate to meet it. What could be done to put them off the scent?

I so well remember how I was brought, one evening, the outlines of a cover plan which was ultimately given the somewhat gruesome name of Operation Mincemeat. I was, I confess, a little dubious whether it would work; but I put it up to the Chiefs of Staff, who approved it in

Foreword

principle. Thereafter, Lieutenant Commander Montagu, who originated the idea, and his colleagues went full steam ahead.

The operation succeeded beyond our wildest dreams. To have spread-eagled the German defensive effort right across Europe, even to the extent of sending German vessels away from Sicily itself, was a remarkable achievement. Those who landed in Sicily, as well as their families, have cause to be especially grateful.

It is not often that the whole story of a secret operation can be made public, told by someone who knows every detail. The military student can be grateful that chance has made it possible for him to have a textbook example of a very specialized branch of the art of war; others will enjoy a real-life thriller—which once more illustrates that truth is stranger than fiction.

Lord Ismay, G.C.B., C.H., D.S.O.

Introduction

"CERTAINLY THE BEST KNOWN, and perhaps the most successful deception operation of the entire war." That is how Sir Michael Howard, the official historian of strategic deception in the Second World War, aptly describes Operation Mincemeat, the story of "the man who never was." It was a bold and imaginative plan, contrived with scrupulous care and executed with skill and courage. Above all it was, as the Chiefs of Staff gleefully reported to Churchill, then visiting Washington, "swallowed whole" by the German intelligence and operations staff. Its indirect result—for deception, like intelligence, can do no more than help toward success—was not only a military victory but the saving of many Allied lives.

It is important to remember that operations of this kind (*opérations d'intoxication* in the colorful French version) do not exist in a vacuum. The false idea that the first Allied landings in Europe would be in the eastern Mediterranean, and not in their self-evident target, Sicily, would not have been planted, or might never have taken root, if German intelligence had not been, as we already knew, predisposed to cherish it. We knew that was so largely from Ultra, the systematic British interception and breaking of

5

Introduction

German high-grade code and cipher signals, of which the number read by Bletchley Park (GCHQ) had passed the impressive total of four thousand a day by early 1943.

It is not surprising that the relatively inefficient Abwehr, the secret intelligence service of the German high command, was ready to swallow it. More importantly the plot hoodwinked the German supreme command itself. From early May 1943 they were thus persuaded to rate the defense of Greece, and even of Sardinia, as more urgent than that of Sicily. Moreover, it was known from Ultra that Hitler personally believed that Greece was the likeliest target. Just as it had helped to suggest Mincemeat, Ultra monitored the consequent orders moving German units. Measures for defending Sardinia and the Greek Peloponnese were to have priority over everything else, two areas on the southwest coast of Greece were specified as likely Allied invasion targets, and the 1st Panzer Division began its laborious journey from France to Greece.

Even two weeks after the actual Allied landings in Sicily, Hitler still felt sure that the main assault would be on Greece. The same phenomenon was repeated a year later. His conviction that the Normandy landings were a sideshow, and that the real attack would come through the Pas de Calais—another notion long fostered by the Allied deception planners—kept important forces (including one first-class unit, the 1st SS Panzer Division) out of the real battle during its most critical period.

Introduction

We now know how widely Mincemeat was appreciated. In late May 1943 General Jodl, head of the German supreme command operations staff, was heard impatiently shouting down the telephone to the German military attaché in Rome: "You can forget about Sicily. We know it's Greece." We may set this against Churchill's remark, made as he approved Mincemeat: "Anyone but a bloody fool would know it was Sicily." Such are the powers of self-persuasion.

Another factor was that the Germans "knew" also that the British forces available were far larger than they really were. That belief had been encouraged by our deception staff for several years, so that every bogus unit, even up to Army size, which they dreamed up found its way eventually into the German Order of Battle and stayed there. By late 1942 German intelligence had assessed the British army as some 45 percent larger than it actually was. That in turn made it easier to suggest that objectives were within our reach, which we knew to be outside it.

It is important to see Mincemeat not as an isolated episode but as part of a long and methodical policy of strategic deception. "Barclay," the overall Mediterranean deception plan for 1943, had four main objects:

To weaken the defenses of Sicily;
To pin down enemy troops in the south of France and the Balkans peninsula;

Introduction

To reduce enemy attacks on our ships as they gathered
for the assault on Sicily; and

To secure the greatest possible surprise for that assault.

All this was carried out on Dudley Clarke's often-quoted principle: "My creed was not 'What do you want the enemy to think?' but 'What do you want him to do?'"

Not all our deception planners met that requirement. In the Far East, Peter Fleming, a man of talent and imagination, sometimes seemed so immersed in the details— the worn briefcase which was soon to be lost with a sheaf of ostensibly secret papers, or the firework display which mimicked the midair explosion of an imaginary aircraft— as to lose sight of his overriding responsibility: to persuade the Japanese to do what we wanted them to do.

Some comments are needed on certain aspects of Mincemeat, which Montagu could not reveal when his book came out in 1953. "George," the man with the wild idea for the operation, could not be named because he stayed on in the secret service. He was Flight-Lieutenant Charles Cholmondeley of Section B1A in MI5, who appears in the story as George. Montagu's account also might never have existed if Duff Cooper's *Operation Heartbreak*, a novel heavily indebted to Mincemeat, had not appeared in 1950, causing an official furor. That might have been followed by Ian Colvin's account of the operation, based on his own research; but it in turn was suppressed by the Joint Intelligence Committee, who decided to fill the gap quickly by asking

Introduction

Montagu to write this account, with its imaginative title.

Several details of the operation probably owed their inspiration to a true event which had taken place in September 1942, some seven months earlier, when an RAF Catalina flying-boat en route for Gibraltar crashed in the sea off Cadiz. It appears that one passenger, a naval officer, was carrying a letter from the American general Mark Clark to the governor of Gibraltar, accepting the latter's invitation to stay at Government House before the Torch landings in North Africa, the proposed date for which was given in the letter. But that letter was later returned by the Spanish authorities "apparently unopened." Clearly, if Mincemeat were to succeed, it must end differently.

It did: choosing the Spanish coast near Huelva, a mere fifty miles away, met all the conditions, as Montagu points out. Not only would the prevailing onshore wind help to drift the body, supported in its Mae West inflatable jacket, toward the beach; an active German agent there, known to be on good terms with local Spanish officials, would be likely to secure copies of the papers himself, or ensure that they quickly reached the Abwehr. Without that, the whole operation would be pointless. His rival in the area, Lieutenant-Commander Gomez-Beare, in the event also succeeded in persuading them that the papers were so important that they must go straight to Berlin—an unusual alliance.

Mincemeat was approved at a meeting of the Twenty (XX or Double-Cross) Committee on 4 February 1943,

9

Introduction

when it was apparently still proposed to drop the body by parachute from an aircraft.

The actual body was dressed in Royal Marines uniform not primarily for the reasons given in chapter five, but because the Germans were believed to have fairly recent copies of the Army list yet were known to have, at most, only the A–L volume of the Navy list, which included the Marines. That information probably derived from our breaking not only of the Abwehr Enigma but also of the ISOS traffic which they also used. ISOS stood for Intelligence Section Oliver Strachey, another group at Bletchley Park.

There was a compelling reason also for taking all possible precautions against a Spanish postmortem examination, and it had nothing to do with pneumonia. The body used was that of an anonymous tramp found in a London warehouse, who had died from mistakenly eating phosphorous rat-poison. If the body were closely examined, that fact would become clear and would virtually eliminate the likelihood of his being a serving officer—thus exposing the deception.

It was to lessen that risk that his wartime identity disc was marked "R/C," he wore a silver cross on a neck-chain, and a St. Christopher plaque was in his wallet: all this in the hope that, when noticed by the Spanish, it would strengthen their traditional religious objection to post-mortem examination.

We must remember that a deception operation that goes wrong is not simply a flop; its wider effects can be disastrous. It focuses enemy attention on precisely what it

Introduction

has tried, but failed, to conceal. If, as Montagu points out, the Germans had discovered that any detail of Mincemeat had been faked, the conclusion would have been clear: the Allies' next target could not be in the Eastern Mediterranean, nor even Sardinia—all subtly indicated in our deception plan. It must be Sicily.

A simple example with a happy ending may demonstrate that point. The Germans painstakingly built a dummy airfield, with dummy aircraft, fuel bowsers, hangars, and control tower all beautifully made of wood, to distract attention from the real airfield not far away. On the day it was completed, the RAF, who had been keeping a quiet eye on it, showed their appreciation by dropping one wooden bomb on it.

I must add a comment on the well-known film version of *The Man Who Never Was*. This is an excellent piece of work in its own right, deservedly popular, dealing with the story imaginatively yet responsibly, and conjuring up the feeling of London in those distant wartime days—and nights. It is therefore important to note where fact ends and fancy begins, not least because it is good fiction, dovetailing imperceptibly into fact.

In brief: Canaris, who appears in Berlin in the film, was really in the Balkans. He had no suspicions, then or later. He made no attempt to check the London end of the story, and so did not send so engaging an Irish agent there, nor anyone else. As far as we know, the "girl in the office," and even her probably imaginary American flat-mate, had no such worry-

Introduction

ing encounters as the film describes. It is a tribute to the scriptwriter, Nigel Balchin, that an audience can accept the whole combined operation of suspense and entertainment so uncritically. Nor do they need to know that the real Montagu appears in the film as one of the critical senior officers at the meeting of the Double-Cross Committee.

Mincemeat itself differs from most deception schemes in depending not on bogus orders, charts, or statistics, but on subtle and apparently irrelevant remarks in three informal letters from and to very senior officers: the principal letter from Nye to Alexander, and the obliquely supporting letters from Mountbatten to Cunningham and Eisenhower. The detailed wording of these splendidly misleading documents hits precisely the right note for their one purpose: the deception of the German intelligence and operations staff at their highest level, about a matter of supreme importance. Their apparently artless plausibility is satisfying in itself. That side of the operation can never be repeated in any recognizable form.

Similarly, the deft personal touches such as Martin's engagement and overdraft, and the letters from his alleged father, bank manager, and—of course—fiancée: these too are more than prosaic window-dressing. Their sheer irrelevance is in itself convincing. They offer the reader some satisfaction through their literary aptness as well as their power to deceive.

It is a privilege to be invited to commend this book. I am grateful to Ralph Erskine, Sir David Hunt, and

Introduction

Edward Thomas, who have given me very useful details. Ralph Bennett helped me by drawing my attention to articles by Roger Morgan and others in *After the Battle* (nos. 54 and 64) which its editor, Winston G. Ramsey, kindly sent me. Three books contain good information and comment on Mincemeat, its purpose, and its consequences: Ralph Bennett, *Ultra and Mediterranean Strategy* (London: Hamish Hamilton, 1989), 222–27; Ralph Bennett, *Behind the Battle* (London: Sinclair-Stevenson, 1994), 202–5; and Michael Howard, *Strategic Deception* (London: HMSO, 1990), 88–93.

Alan Stripp

Author's Note

THIS IS A TRUE ACCOUNT of an operation carried out in the years 1942–43. Such facts as are not within my own personal knowledge are derived from contemporary documents and reports, and are neither based on anyone's recollection of what happened ten years ago nor on anyone's attempts to justify his actions or those of his associates.

I naturally could not speak or write about it until a fictional story partially based on this operation, and references in German memoirs to the receipt of the documents which formed the basis of this deception, made it clear that it would no longer be possible to maintain that secrecy which all of us who took part in the operation had preserved. This fact was recognized by the authorities, who doubtless appreciated the possible dangers and disadvantages which might result from publication by partially informed writers, and I was given official permission to publish the full story.

The operation was carried out by a team who must, unfortunately, remain anonymous as some of them are still in government service. Therefore I have substituted a false Christian name for "George's" real one; I have also, of course, maintained the secrecy of "Major Martin's"

Author's Note

identity. Where I have referred to other persons I have used the titles and ranks that they held at the time of the operation.

If anyone studies this story, some good may result. Perhaps, when some "leakage" of a secret document is reported, the public may not be so ready as they have been to blame our security services; they may wonder whether the security services have been stupid—or clever?

I must record my thanks to Lord Ismay for his help in 1942 and 1943 and for writing the foreword, as well as to Jack Garbutt of the *Sunday Express* for his great kindness and for the wise advice which he gave me on this, my first, excursion into authorship.

I wish to acknowledge my deep indebtedness to all my colleagues, without whose loyal help and brilliant inventiveness there could have been no Operation Mincemeat. And also my indebtedness to Viscount Norwich, without whose unwitting assistance there could have been no publication of this story.

16

1 The Birth of an Idea

IN THE GRAVEYARD of the Spanish town of Huelva there lies a British subject. As he died, alone, in the foggy damp of England in the late autumn of 1942, he little thought that he would lie forever under the sunny skies of Spain after a funeral with full military honours, nor that he would, after death, render a service to the Allies that saved many hundreds of British and American lives. In life he had done little for his country; but in death he did more than most could achieve by a lifetime of service.

*　*　*　*　*

It all really started through a wild idea of George's. He and I were members of a small inter-Service and inter-departmental committee which used to meet weekly to deal with questions of the security of intended operations. We exchanged and discussed information that had been obtained from all kinds of sources—from our own Services and other sources at home as well as from neutral countries, together with Intelligence reports from enemy countries. With all this and the latest information as to Allied "intentions" —not only immediate and probable, but also "long-term possible"—we had to try to detect any leakages that might have occurred and any "intelligent anticipation" that the enemy might already have made, and also to guard against such leakages and anticipations in the future.

It was not an easy task, but the committee was a good one: it comprised not only Regular officers of considerable knowledge and experience, but also temporary officers and civilians with most varied backgrounds; we were a mixed lot, and between us we could view any item of information as it would strike observers from any walk of life; we had a thoroughly variegated fund of knowledge and there were few spheres of activity with which we had no contacts.

George produced his idea during a discussion over a report with which we had been supplied from occupied Europe; as happened from time to time, we were puzzled whether it was genuine or had been planted by the Germans for transmission to the Allies.

George had one of those subtle and ingenious minds which is forever throwing up fantastic ideas— mostly so ingenious as either to be impossible of implementation or so intricate as to render their efficacy problematical, but every now and again quite brilliant

18

The Birth of an Idea

in their simplicity. As we puzzled whether this particular report was genuine, or whether the Germans had captured the agent concerned and were sending reports through him or for him, George remembered a recent warning that had been issued reminding officers that it was forbidden for secret documents to be carried in aircraft lest they should be shot down in enemy territory.

Starting from that, George suddenly suggested that as a check on such reports we should try to get the Germans to plant something on us that we knew was planted, so that we could see what their line was and how they put it over: if we could drop a resistance workers' wireless set into France (he suggested) and it started working it would be difficult to tell whether the Germans or a friendly Frenchman was working it, but if it dropped accompanied by a dead body attached to a badly opened parachute, the task of checking might be easier. A Frenchman would probably tell us what had occurred, whereas the Germans would be more likely to conceal what had happened and work the set as if the agent was still alive. It would not be certain, but it did not involve much effort and might be worth trying. "Does anyone know whether we can get a body?" asked George.

This was not one of his better inspirations, and we rapidly demolished it; agents did not carry their codes or their routine and system for sending messages with

19

them for anyone to find, so how would the Germans transmit messages?

Also, if a parachute failed, whatever was hanging from it would be bound to hit the ground with a considerable bump; if it was a body, this would almost certainly result in a broken limb as well as grazes and scratches, and injuries inflicted after death can always be detected. There was therefore no hope of dropping a dead body attached to a partially opened parachute without the finder being able to tell that the body had been dead for some time before it hit the ground. Besides, even if we could get a dead body (and no one knew whether we could), our field of choice would indeed be limited if it had to be that of someone who had died through falling from a height! No; this was one of George's failures, and we quickly turned back to our report: was it genuine or not? But some months later George's wild idea produced results.

By the summer of 1942 our little committee was in the midst of its first big job. "Operation Torch," the invasion of North Africa, was being mounted, and the experience that we had gained in trying to guard the security of small-scale operations, involving relatively few units, was receiving its first full test.

In spite of all that could be done in the way of security, it was obviously impossible to prevent the enemy knowing that something was brewing. In the first place, it was apparent to everyone that the Allies would not just sit back indefinitely: there must be an invasion somewhere. Secondly, there could be no restriction on foreign diplomats: they moved around the country and they met and spoke to people, not only people in the know, but also some of the thousands who were bound to see the congregation of ships or of troops before they left this country; and whatever view had to be taken officially, none of us had any illusions as to the neutrality of a number of diplomats. Besides, even a pro-British diplomat had a job to do: he had to report to his Government what was going on over here, and once the report got to his country there could be no doubt that there would be at least one official or minister over there who was either paid, or at any rate ideologically ready, to pass the information on to the Germans. Thirdly, there were neutral business-men and sailors travelling between this country and the Continent.

Therefore we could not hope to prevent the Germans knowing that there *was* an operation afoot. What we could hope to do was to prevent the vital information of "When?" and "Where?" leaking.

Until the invasion of North Africa had taken place the Allies had no presumptive foothold on the continent of Europe, and the war in North Africa consisted of a campaign in which we were pushing from east to west with our armies based on the Suez Canal Zone. As a result of this situation there was no reason why the Allies should not make an attack at almost any point. As far as the Germans knew, we might land in Norway, in the Low Countries or in France, or try to push up through Spain; we might seize the Canaries or the Azores to help in the war against U-boats; or we might land in Libya to attack Rommel's army in its rear. Except in Egypt, we were wholly uncommitted, and any place in German-held Europe or neutral countries was open to assault.

In these circumstances all that it was necessary for our committee to try to ensure, when we attacked Dieppe or the Lofoten Islands or planned any other assault, was that the actual target and date did not get over to the enemy. That involved nothing more than leaking a false target to the troops concerned, perhaps backing such leaks up with papers about an issue of sun helmets—if they were in fact going to the Lofoten Islands—or something of that kind, and then working really hard to reduce, as much as possible, the bits of information which would inevitably get out of this country. In other words, our principle was to try to make security as complete as possible, and then try to prevent any leakage that *did* get by our precautions being such as would give away the true target.

When "Operation Torch" was being launched against North Africa we could still operate on this basis and, as we studied our Intelligence reports and learned of the movements that the Germans made, we realised that this system had worked as the potential targets were so many that the Germans could not get a definite idea even of where we would strike.

But our problem would be entirely different after "Operation Torch" had been completed. At that stage of the war the Allies would have command of the whole of the North African coast and would be poised ready to strike at what the Prime Minister called "the soft under-belly of Europe." Our committee was kept in touch with the strategic thinking of our Chiefs of Staff and also with that of the Americans. We knew that there were some differences of opinion, but there was a definite probability that we would strike there, and our committee had to be prepared to play our part when the Allies attacked.

With the whole North African coast in Allied hands it was pretty obvious that we would not turn round and transport all those troops back to England for an invasion of France across the Channel, and at least some of them were bound to be used across the Mediterranean. They could form part of an army for the the conquest of Italy or they could be used for landing in the South of France or in Greece. Any one of these campaigns was a possibility, and our committee had to be prepared to deal with whatever might eventually be decided upon. We might perhaps have been able to cope with this task on the system which had

worked so well up till then had that been the whole
story, but there was one feature of the strategic situation which created a new problem.

Sicily lay in the middle of the Mediterranean like a
football at the toe of Italy, and until it had been captured the passing of a convoy through the Mediterranean was a major operation attended by enormous
losses, and this situation would remain even when the
airfields in North Africa were finally in our hands. It
was made clear to our committee that the reduction
of Sicily would almost certainly have to be undertaken
before any of the other operations could take place.
As we always had to make our preparations long before
an operation was launched, we were considering this
next job, the security of the invasion of Sicily, even
before "Torch" was finally mounted.

And here we foresaw trouble. If Sicily was a clear
probability to us, once North Africa was in Allied
hands, it would be just as clear a probability to the
Germans. Indeed, as the Prime Minister eventually
said, when approving this operation of ours, it did not
matter taking some risk of revealing Sicily as the target,
as "anybody but a damn' fool would *know* it is Sicily."
How would we be able, when the time came, to prevent the Germans from reinforcing the defences of Sicily to a dangerous extent as the result of the same
strategic reasoning which had caused the Allies to attack it?

The Birth of an Idea

As we were puzzling over this problem, the penny suddenly dropped, and George's fantastic idea of some time before justified itself. "Why," I said, "shouldn't we get a body, disguise it as a staff officer, and give him really high-level papers which will show clearly that we are going to attack somewhere else. We won't have to drop him on land, as the aircraft might have come down in the sea on the way round to the Med. He would float ashore with the papers either in France or in Spain; it won't matter which. Probably Spain would be best, as the Germans wouldn't have as much chance to examine the body there as if they got it into their own hands, while it's certain that they will get the documents, or at least copies." So the idea was born. Excitedly, we discussed its potentialities. We would have to check on a number of points: What sort of condition would a body be in after an aircraft crash in the sea? What were the usual causes of death in such cases? What would a *post mortem* reveal? Could we get a suitable body—indeed, could we get *any* body? Such were the first questions to which we would have to get answers. If those were satisfactory the plan was worth studying with care, for we none of us doubted that, given the chance, the Spaniards would play the part for which we had cast them, and then what a chance we would have given ourselves!

2 Preliminary Enquiries

WE HAD TALKED GLIBLY of "getting a body," but we had realised that there would be difficulties; we had yet to learn how difficult it would actually be. None of us, indeed, entirely liked the idea, for even in the stress of war one's natural respect for the sanctity of the human body remains a powerful instinct. But for us that instinct was overborne by a realisation of the lives that could be saved by the temporary use of a body that we were confident would eventually receive a proper and decent burial. The difficulty with which we were immediately faced was that imposed by security. How could we go to relatives in their hour of sorrow and ask to be allowed to take without explanation the remains of the son or husband or brother whom they mourned? And if we had to explain, what could we say? In fiction one could, perhaps, expect that we would meet a man who happened to be the sole relative of someone who had just died a death suitable for our plan—a man of that rare type who would just agree

26

to our taking the body and would ask no questions as to why we wanted it. In fiction, perhaps, but not in real life!

Before we started our search, we had first to make sure what kind of body we needed. If the Germans were to accept the body as that of the victim of an aircraft crash at sea, we would have to present them with someone whose body did not afford signs of a cause of death inconsistent with that.

It seemed to me that the best approach to this question would be from the point of view of the man who would do the *post mortem*. What would a pathologist expect to find and what would he expect not to find in the body of a man who had drifted ashore after an aircraft had been lost at sea? For, after all, the aircraft need not have actually crashed.

My thoughts at once turned to Sir Bernard Spilsbury. No one had more experience of pathology than he had, and I felt that no better security risk existed: one could be certain that he at any rate would not gossip or even pass what I said to him on "in confidence to someone whom he could trust." In this respect, there had never been any difference between Sir Bernard and an oyster. And he had one even rarer quality: I felt sure that he would not ask any questions other than those needed for the solution of the problem put to him: *he* would just take the fact that we wanted the Germans and Spaniards to accept a floating body as that of a victim of an aircraft disaster, and would neither ask me why nor seek to find an answer elsewhere.

So I rang up Sir Bernard and we arranged a meeting at his club, the Junior Carlton. There, over a glass of sherry, I put our problem to him. After a moment or two of thought, he gave me one of those concise, yet complete, expositions that had convinced so many juries—and even so many judges. His advice gave me hope. If the body was floating in a "Mae West" when it was recovered, we could use one of a man who had either drowned or died from any but a few of the "natural causes"; victims of an aircraft disaster at sea sometimes died from an injury received in the crash, and some died from drowning, but many died from exposure or even from shock; our field of search was less narrow than I had feared it might be.

My opinion of Sir Bernard was fully justified; that extraordinary man listened to my questions and gave me his answers without ever for a moment giving vent to the curiosity which he must have felt. He asked me some questions which bore on the pathological problem that I was putting to him, but never once did he ask why I wanted to know or what I was proposing to do.

But even then the quest was not easy. We could not make any open enquiries—at all costs we had to avoid anything which might start talk. We could not risk

28

anyone remembering that someone had been trying to
obtain a dead body, and such a search was just the sort
of thing that is likely to start gossip: "Have you heard?
It's frightfully odd. So-and-So was asking Such-and-
Such the other day where he could get a dead body."
And so, very quietly, our search went on. There we
were, in 1942, surrounded all too often by dead bodies,
but none that we could take. We felt like the Ancient
Mariner—bodies, bodies, everywhere, nor any one to
take! We felt like Pirandello—"Six officers in search of
a corpse."

At one time we feared that we might have to do a
body-snatch—"do a Burke and Hare" as one of us put
it; but we did not like that idea, if we could possibly
avoid it. We managed to make some very guarded enquiries from a few Service medical officers whom we
could trust; but when we heard of a possibility, either
the relatives were unlikely to agree or we could not
trust those whose permission we would need not to
mention to other close relatives what had happened—
or there were some other snags, such as a complication
in the cause of death.

At last, when we had begun to feel that it would
have either to be a "Burke and Hare" after all or we
would have to extend our enquiries so widely as to
risk suspicion of our motives turning into gossip, we
heard of someone who had just died from pneumonia
after exposure: pathologically speaking, it looked as if

The Man Who Never Was

he might answer our requirements. We made feverish enquiries into his past and about his relatives; we were soon satisfied that these would not talk or pass on such information as we could give them. But there was still the crucial question: could we get permission to use the body without saying what we proposed to do with it and why? All we could possibly tell anyone was that we could guarantee that the purpose would be a really worthwhile one, as anything that was done would be with approval on the highest level, and that the remains would eventually receive proper burial, though under a false name.

Permission, for which our indebtedness is great, was obtained on condition that I should never let it be known whose corpse it was. It must therefore suffice for me to say that the body was that of a young man in his early thirties. He had not been very physically fit for some time before his death, but we could accept that for, as I said to a senior officer who queried the point, "He does not have to look like an officer—only like a staff officer."

As a precaution, I had another chat with Sir Bernard Spilsbury. He was quite satisfied: the pneumonia was a help, for there would tend to be some liquid in the lungs, as might well be the case if the man had died while floating in a rough sea. If a *post mortem* examination was made by someone who had formed the preconceived idea that the death was probably due to drowning there was little likelihood that the difference between this liquid, in lungs that had started to decompose, and sea water would be noticed. Sir Bernard closed our talk with the characteristically confident statement: "You have nothing to fear from a Spanish *post mortem;* to detect that this young man had not died after an aircraft had been lost at sea would need a pathologist of my experience—and there aren't any in Spain."

So we arranged for the body to be kept in suitable cold storage until we were ready for it.

3 "Operation Mincemeat"

I NOW HAD TO GET general approval for the principle of the operation. The first step, as always before any operation, was to get a code name; except in the case of a few major operations for which the Prime Minister himself invented the names, these were always taken from lists issued by us to the Service departments and the various Commands. I therefore went to see what names had been allocated for Admiralty use, and there I found that the word "Mincemeat" had just been restored after employment in a successful operation some time before. My sense of humour having by this time become somewhat macabre, the word seemed to be one of good omen—and "Operation Mincemeat" it became.

I had next to decide where we were to send the body, and I chose Huelva as the best destination, if delivery there was possible. For we knew that there was a very active German agent at Huelva who had excellent contacts with certain Spaniards, both officials and others. If the body reached Huelva, the odds were very heavy that this agent would be given any papers or other objects of importance that might be with it; even if circumstances prevented that happening, there was no doubt whatsoever that he would either get copies or be given detailed information, and we could then be sure that he would alert his superiors in Madrid who would intercept the documents at a higher level. Our only risk was that the body and papers would be handed straight over to the British Vice-Consul so quickly that no one could intercept anything. But the co-operation between the Spaniards and the Germans was so complete that such a proper procedure was most improbable: if there were a Spaniard who proposed to do that, I had little doubt but that there would be several others who would step in and prevent it.

Huelva had a further advantage in that it was not too near to Gibraltar; we did not want the Spaniards to send the body for burial there. The arrival at Gibraltar of the body of an officer who did not really exist might give rise to talk which would be almost certain to be picked up by the many German agents who obtained information through the Spaniards who entered and left that area each day.

So I went to the Hydrographer of the Navy at the Admiralty and made some enquiries about weather and tidal conditions at various points off the coast of Spain at various times of the year. Our luck was holding. Although the tidal stream would not be too helpful and would set along the coast, the southwesterly wind, which would be the prevailing wind in April, would be "onshore." Indeed, the Hydrographer thought that "an object" would probably drift in towards the shore, and a body in a "Mae West" would be comparatively more affected by the wind than would the sort of object which I had led him to envisage.

So Huelva was decided on. There was practically no doubt that the body would float inshore: then, if the normal procedure was followed, the body would be handed over to the British Vice-Consul for burial. And, as I have said, we were confident that the efficiency of the local German agent would ensure that any papers, or at least copies of them, would eventually reach the Germans. Our confidence in him was not misplaced.

While we were going into the exact location for "Mincemeat's" arrival, a means of transportation had to be devised. He could not be dropped for fear of injury, which left three methods of placing him in the sea: submarine, flying boat or a temporary diversion of one of the ships which escorted the convoys up the coast of Spain. Of these a submarine could clearly get much the closest inshore without risk of detection. I therefore asked permission from the Vice-Chief of Naval Staff (Home) to discuss possibilities with Admiral Barry, the Flag Officer commanding our submarines: it was, of course, on the basis that our planning

"Operation Mincemeat"

was purely tentative, so that a complete scheme could be worked out for submission to the Chiefs of Staff.

Admiral Barry readily saw the possibilities of the idea, and I had a preliminary talk with his Chief Staff Officer. He decided that "Mincemeat" could be carried in a submarine on passage to Malta, as these quite frequently took important but not too bulky articles to that island. We discussed whether the body should be transported in the casing (that is under what would normally be called the deck) or inside the actual pressure hull of the submarine. In spite of the size of the container, which would have to be some 6 feet 6 inches long and about 2 feet in diameter, he considered that it could be accommodated inside the pressure hull and brought up through the conning tower for launching at sea. This greatly eased our problem, as it meant that we would only have to get an airtight canister and not a pressure-proof container, which would have had to be much heavier and more complicated. The question remained whether the body could be kept in a plain canister for the necessary time, after removal from cold storage, without decomposition being too great—or would we have to try to get some form of enormous thermos flask?

So I consulted Sir Bernard Spilsbury once more. He took the view that temperature would be of comparatively minor importance if the body was really cold when it was put into the container. The important thing was to exclude as much oxygen as possible, as it was that which hastened decomposition. He advised that the best method for us to use would be to stand our container on one end and fill it with dry ice; as that melted into carbon dioxide, it would prevent air from entering. We should then lower the body carefully into the canister and pack it round once more with dry ice. If that was done carefully, there should be little oxygen left in the container, and the rate of decomposition would be so slowed down that, if the body was picked up shortly after launching, its condition would be consistent with a few days' immersion floating in from an aircraft crash some distance offshore.

So we arranged for a container to be made of two skins of 22-gauge sheet steel welded together, with asbestos wool between the skins; at the top there was a similar lid which was bedded on to an airtight rubber gasket by sixteen nuts; a box-spanner was chained to the lid, to which it was clipped when not in use; a lifting handle was provided at each end, for it would weigh over 400 pounds with the body inside.

To complete the account of this part of our preparations, I should record that later on I saw Admiral Barry again and told him that the plan was going ahead and that, if we got final approval, we would want the operation carried out at about the end of April. This would also have the advantage from the submarine's point of view of there being little or no

moon, so as to render detection close inshore less likely.
He decided that H.M. Submarine *Seraph* might be
used, as she could delay her departure for Malta by a
fortnight, spending the time "working up" in home
waters. The chance of using *Seraph* was fortunate, as
she was commanded by Lieutenant Jewell, and he and
his ship's company had already had experience of special operations in connection with the North Africa
landings; they had picked up General Giraud on his
escape from captivity and it was they who had put
General Mark Clark ashore on the coast of North
Africa when he made secret contact with the French,
and then taken him off again.

I had prepared tentative "operation orders" for the
Captain of the submarine, and these Admiral Barry approved; but, at his suggestion, Lieutenant Jewell came
to the Flag Officer, Submarines Headquarters, where
he and I could talk over the whole matter.

I gave him the "operation orders," which were as
follows:

OPERATION MINCEMEAT

1. *Object*
To cause a briefcase containing documents to drift ashore
as near as possible to HUELVA in Spain in such circumstances
that it will be thought to have been washed ashore from an
aircraft which crashed at sea when the case was being taken
by an officer from the U.K. to Allied Forces H.Q. in North
Africa.

37

The Man Who Never Was

2. *Method*

A dead body dressed in the battledress uniform of a Major, Royal Marines, and wearing a "Mae West," will be taken out in a submarine, together with the briefcase and a rubber dinghy.

The body will be packed fully clothed and ready (and wrapped in a blanket to prevent friction) in a tubular air-tight container (which will be labeled as "Optical Instruments").

The container is just under 6 feet 6 inches long and just under 2 feet in diameter and has no excrescences of any kind on the sides. The end which opens has a flush-fitting lid which is held tightly in position by a number of nuts and has fitted on its exterior in clips a box-spanner with a permanent tommy-bar which is chained to the lid.

Both ends are fitted with handles which fold down flat. It will be possible to lift the container by using both handles or even by using the handle in the lid alone, but it would be better not to take the whole weight on the handle at the other end, as the steel of which the container is made is of light gauge to keep the weight as low as possible. The approximate total weight when the container is full will be 400 pounds.

When the container is closed the body will be packed round with a certain amount of dry ice. The container should therefore be opened on deck, as the dry ice will give off carbon dioxide.

3. *Position*

The body should be put into the water as close inshore as prudently possible and as near to HUELVA as possible, preferably to the north-west of the river mouth.

"Operation Mincemeat"

According to the Hydrographic Department, the tides in that area run mainly up and down the coast, and every effort should therefore be made to choose a period with an onshore wind. South-westerly winds are in fact the prevailing winds in that area at this time of year.

The latest information about the tidal streams in that area, as obtained from the Superintendent of Tides, is attached.

4. *Delivery of the Package*

The package will be brought up to the port of departure by road on whatever day is desired, preferably as close to the sailing day as possible. The briefcase will be handed over at the same time to the Captain of the submarine. The rubber dinghy will also be a separate parcel.

5. *Disposal of.the Body*

When the body is removed from the container all that will be necessary will be to fasten the chain attached to the briefcase through the belt of the trench-coat, which will be the outer garment on the body. The chain is of the type worn under the coat, round the chest and out through the sleeve. At the end is a "dog-lead" type of clip for attaching to the handle of the briefcase and a similar clip for forming the loop round the chest. It is this loop that should be made through the belt of the trench-coat as if the officer has slipped the chain off for comfort in the aircraft, but has nevertheless kept it attached to him so that the bag should not either be forgotten or slide away from him in the aircraft.

The body should then be deposited in the water, as should also be the rubber dinghy. As this should drift at a different speed from the body, the exact position at which

39

it is released is unimportant, but it should be near the body, but not too near if that is possible.

6. *Those in the Know at Gibraltar*

Steps have been taken to inform F.O.IC.[1] Gibraltar and his S.O.(I).[2] No one else there will be in the picture.

7. *Signals*

If the operation is successfully carried out, a signal should be made "MINCEMEAT completed." If that is made from Gibraltar the S.O.(I) should be asked to send it addressed to D.N.I.[3] (PERSONAL). If it can be made earlier it should be made in accordance with orders from F.O.S.[4]

8. *Cancellation*

If the operation has to be cancelled a signal will be made "Cancel MINCEMEAT." In that case the body and container should be sunk in deep water; as the container may have positive buoyancy, it may either have to be weighted or water may have to be allowed to enter. In the latter case care must be taken that the body does not escape. The briefcase should be handed to the S.O.(I) at Gibraltar, with instructions to burn the contents unopened, if there is no possibility of taking that course earlier. The rubber dinghy should be handed to the S.O.(I) for disposal.

9. *Abandonment*

If the operation has to be abandoned, a signal should be made "MINCEMEAT abandoned" as soon as possible (see Para. 7 above).

---

[1] Flag Officer in Charge.
[2] Staff Officer, Intelligence.
[3] Director of Naval Intelligence.
[4] Flag Officer, Submarines (Admiral Barry).

"Operation Mincemeat"

10. *Cover*

This is a matter for consideration. Until the operation actually takes place, it is thought that the labelling of the container "Optical Instruments" will provide sufficient cover. It is suggested that the cover after the operation has been completed should be that it is hoped to trap a very active German agent in this neighbourhood, and it is hoped that sufficient evidence can be obtained by this means to get the Spaniards to eject him. The importance of dealing with this man should be impressed on the crew, together with the fact that any leakage that may *ever* take place about this will compromise our power to get the Spaniards to act in such cases; also that they will never learn whether we were successful in this objective, as the whole matter will have to be conducted in secrecy with the Spaniards or we won't be able to get them to act.

It is in fact most important that the Germans and Spaniards should accept these papers in accordance with Para. I. If they should suspect that the papers are a "plant," it might have far-reaching consequences of great magnitude.

> (*Signed*) E. E. S. MONTAGU,
> *Lt.-Cdr., R.N.V.R.*
> 31.3.43.

We then discussed the operation and filled in points of detail.

While all these things were being arranged, we had been busy over the more interesting matters. What document could we provide which could be so impressive that it would make the Germans alter their planning and disposition of forces? How could we provide the document with a sufficiently convincing background to make them accept it as genuine; for Pooh-Bah was right when he spoke of " . . . corroborative detail, intended to give artistic verisimilitude to an otherwise bald and unconvincing narrative."

4 The Vital Document

ONE THING seemed to me to be crystal clear: if the purpose of this document was to deceive the Germans *so that they would act upon it,* then it had to be on a really high level; no indiscretion or "leak" from an officer of normal rank would do. Even a security lapse from one brigadier, air commodore or rear-admiral to another would not be weighty enough.

If the German General Staff was to be persuaded, in face of all probabilities, to bank on our next target being somewhere other than Sicily, it would have to have before it a document which was passing between officers who *must* know what our real plans were, who could not possibly be mistaken and who could not themselves be the victims of a cover plan. If the operation was to be worthwhile, I had to have a document written by someone, and to someone, whom the Germans knew—and whom they knew to be "right in the know."

So I put up the proposal that General Sir Archibald

The Man Who Never Was

Nye, the Vice-Chief of the Imperial General Staff, should write the letter—and that he should write it to General Alexander (who commanded an army in Tunisia, under General Eisenhower) at 18th Army Group Headquarters. The letter should be of what we junior officers called "the old boy type"; it should be on the lines of "Look here, old chap, I want you to understand that we realise your problems, but we have our difficulties too. The C.I.G.S.[1] has had to turn down some of your requests, although you're pressing for them. There really are reasons why you can't have what you want just now, and here they are. . . ." and so on: the sort of friendly letter which can give information and explanations that can't be put into an official communication. That sort of letter, and that sort of letter only, could convey convincingly to the Germans the indication that our next target was not Sicily, and yet could be found in the possession of an officer and not in a bag full of the usual official documents going from home to our army abroad.

I was aiming high—and I had to. I expected something of an explosion—and I got it! For many of even the most able and efficient people failed to appreciate what was wanted for this sort of job; for to realise that needed a particular sort of approach and a peculiar sort of mind that could look at the same puzzle from several different angles at the same time.

[1] Chief of the Imperial General Staff.

The Vital Document

You are a British Intelligence officer; you have an opposite number in the enemy Intelligence, say (as in the last war), in Berlin; and above him is the German Operational Command. What you, a Briton with a British background, think can be deduced from a document does not matter. It is what *your opposite number,* with his German knowledge and background, will think that matters—what construction *he* will put on the document. Therefore, if you want *him* to think such-and-such a thing, you must give him something which will make *him* (and not *you*) think it. But he may be suspicious and want confirmation; you must think out what enquiries will *he* make (not what enquiries would *you* make) and give him the answers to those enquiries so as to satisfy him. In other words, you must remember that a German does not think and react as an Englishman does, and you must put yourself into his mind.

But you must not forget the Operational Staff to whom he reports and whom he has to convince if you are to succeed in your plot. The German Operational Staff does not know all the Allied difficulties—for example, how short you are of, say, landing-craft—and they may be prepared to believe that an operation is possible which your own Operational Staff know is not on the cards at all; you have to remember that your plan has to deceive *them,* and not your own Staff. But it is not everyone who can remember, *and apply,* those considerations.

And so we ran into difficulties. But before I record them I should say a word or two about "cover targets" and "cover plans." If you are to prevent there being a concentration at your target ready to meet your landing you must try to draw the enemy's defensive effort and forces elsewhere; if possible, he should be convinced that you won't attack your real target, but will attack somewhere else—that you will attack what we called the "cover target." As I have already mentioned, it is usually certain that there will be some leakage that an operation is intended, and the security measures designed to prevent such leakage giving away the real target may sometimes be adapted to fulfil a second purpose also—to help to put over the cover target. For instance, if any leakage did occur about the operation which I have instanced against the Lofoten Islands, and if sun helmets had been issued, the leakage might well be such that the enemy would deduce that the target was somewhere tropical. If the ships which were to transport the troops received charts or other information which indicated the chosen cover target (let us say Dakar), the various leakages which reached the Germans from those and other factors might well be added together by the German Intelligence Service to make the picture that you wanted them to have.

The best possible cover target would be one so far

away from the real one that any sea, air or land defences that the enemy might prepare would be well
clear of the real target. To give an exaggerated example: if you were going to invade North Africa and
could persuade the enemy that you were going into
Norway (oh, what a happy dream!), any extra defences that he put into Norway could not possibly in-
terfere with your real operation.

But in actual war the cover target may have to be
in the same general area as the real target, and then it
is impossible to divert the whole of the enemy's defences. For instance, if at the time of our North Africa
landings in 1942 we had put over a cover target of a
landing in Rommel's rear at, say, Tobruk—and if we had
succeeded in convincing the Germans—we might have
succeeded in diverting some military forces and perhaps
the Luftwaffe to that area, but the U-boats would have
been drawn to the Straits of Gibraltar through which
the real convoys would have to pass for the genuine
operation. Often, therefore, it is the case of a compromise between what would be a perfect cover target
and what it is possible to get the enemy to believe.

When we came to relate this theory to the particular
problem which faced our Intelligence team, our task
was to try to convince the Germans that we were not
going to attack Sicily—the target which must have been
obvious to them—and to persuade them to move their

forces elsewhere and to use up time and effort in strengthening the defences of other places.

Looking at the situation from the Allied angle, we had an army under General Eisenhower based on French North Africa at the western end of the Mediterranean and another army under Field-Marshal Sir Henry Wilson based on Egypt, together holding the whole North Africa coast. We knew that it was intended that both these great forces should be used for a single operation. There were many reasons for this decision which it would take too long to detail here, but I can summarize them in brief by saying that an assault on the defended coast of Sicily, followed by an advance up the peninsula of Italy, would need all the forces that we had available. Apart from the actual troops and aircraft engaged, there was a considerable shortage of landing-craft and the task of providing the shipping and escorts necessary to supply and maintain the campaign would preclude the conduct of two campaigns at once.

When we looked at the same problem from the German viewpoint, the picture was somewhat different. So far as they knew, the Allies could use General Eisenhower's army in the western Mediterranean to attack the South of France, although this would probably necessitate the reduction of Sicily, Sardinia and Corsica, and would be a risky operation with Italy as an unconquered base for counterattacks on the flank of our supply lines. Equally, the same army or the army based on Egypt could be used for an attack on Italy, although, if the western army was to be used for this purpose, it would almost certainly necessitate the conquest of Sicily as a first step. Finally the eastern army could be used for an invasion of Greece and an advance through the Balkans.

There was no reason to believe that the Germans knew of our shortage of landing-craft, and it was quite possible that they could be led to believe that we were going to mount two operations, one in the western Mediterranean with General Eisenhower's army and one in the eastern Mediterranean with Sir Henry Wilson's army.

When our team considered the deception that we wanted to convey by "Operation Mincemeat," we reasoned as follows: as the Allies had most of their forces in Tunisia, it was hopeless to try to persuade the Germans that we would take our convoys from there through the narrows past their airfields in Sicily. Therefore, any cover target would have to be somewhere west of Italy if the Germans were to believe that it represented the operation in which these troops were involved. Sardinia had already been chosen as the official cover target so as to pretend that we were going to by-pass Sicily and take Sardinia and Corsica, thus opening the whole of the coast of Italy and southern France to attack.

But it seemed to me that, as we would not have to rely on a series of leaks which might or might not reach the Germans, but could use a single document, there could be a second string to our bow. I felt that we could probably convince the Germans that Sir Henry Wilson's army under General Montgomery was not going to take part in the same operation as General Eisenhower's, and that it was going to conduct an invasion of Greece and an advance up the Balkans. There did not seem to be any reason why they should not be led to believe in a double operation with an assault at each end of the Mediterranean, and if we could succeed in convincing them of this we could get a much wider dispersal of their forces than if we based our deception only on the "official" cover target of Sardinia.

I therefore proposed that the letter to General Alexander should reveal that there were to be two operations: his, under General Eisenhower's command, against Sardinia and perhaps Corsica, with another under Field-Marshal Sir Henry Wilson against Greece. I suggested also that the letter should reveal that we were going to *try to convince the Germans that we were going to invade Sicily!* It seemed to me that the beauty of this was that if there were any actual leakage of our real plans, the Germans would think that what was in fact a leakage was only part of the cover that they had read about in the letter. If they swallowed our deception—that one letter—they would disbelieve any genuine information that might leak through.

So the proposal was put up to the Chiefs of Staff—and then the trouble started! Not many people saw the proposal, for the "usual channels" were by-passed; but even then, as the plan and the rough draft of the document went up and down to the Chiefs of Staff and back again, everyone who felt himself to be an expert, and to know the German mind, had bright ideas. It was too dangerous, they said, to try for high stakes, and the letter should be a low-level one, merely putting over a false date; we would never get the Germans to swallow the story and we would be bound to pinpoint Sicily; we must not mention Sardinia as the supposed real target, as, if the Germans saw through the deception, *that* would pinpoint Sicily.

Perhaps the greatest achievement of the whole operation was to persuade our masters that this was an opportunity that would never recur, and that if we were to achieve a real success we must aim high. I have little doubt, as I look back, that to deceive the German High Command was nothing like as difficult as it was to persuade their British opposite numbers that we could do that.

Fortunately, after a while, Sir Archibald Nye himself got really intrigued; he tried a letter, based on my draft, which he suggested might do. It had to be

51

pointed out that, although it indicated the cover targets in just the right sort of way, it would be wholly unconvincing; it was the sort of straightforward letter which could and would go in an official bag and would never be given to an officer to carry in his pocket. This was a challenge to which Sir Archibald rose wonderfully, and he produced a truly magnificent letter. To help the deception, in case the Germans heard of "Husky" (the real code name for the invasion of Sicily), he used that as the code name for the eastern operation against Greece, and used "Brimstone," a fake code name, for the western operation against Sardinia. His draft ran as follows:

Telephone: Whitehall 9400.
Chief of the Imperial
General Staff.

War Office,
Whitehall,
London, S.W.1.
23rd April, 1943.

Personal and Most Secret

MY DEAR ALEX,

I am taking advantage of sending you a personal letter by hand of one of Mountbatten's officers, to give you the inside history of our recent exchange of cables about Mediterranean operations and their attendant cover plans. You may have felt our decisions were somewhat arbitrary, but I can assure you in fact that the C.O.S. Committee [1] gave the most careful consideration both to your recommendation and also to Jumbo's.[2]

[1] Chiefs of Staff Committee.
[2] Nickname of Field-Marshal Sir Henry Wilson, Commander-in-Chief, Middle East.

The Vital Document

We have had recent information that the Boche have been reinforcing and strengthening their defences in Greece and Crete and C.I.G.S. felt that our forces for the assault were insufficient. It was agreed by the Chiefs of Staff that the 5th Division should be reinforced by one Brigade Group for the assault on the beach south of CAPE ARAXOS and that a similar reinforcement should be made for the 56th Division at KALAMATA. We are earmarking the necessary forces and shipping.

Jumbo Wilson had proposed to select SICILY as cover target for "HUSKY"; but we have already chosen it as cover for operation "BRIMSTONE." The C.O.S. Committee went into the whole question exhaustively again and came to the conclusion that in view of the preparations in Algeria, the amphibious training which will be taking place on the Tunisian coast and the heavy air bombardment which will be put down to neutralise the Sicilian airfields, we should stick to our plan of making it cover for "BRIMSTONE"—indeed, we stand a very good chance of making him think we will go for Sicily—it is an obvious objective and one about which he must be nervous. On the other hand, they felt there wasn't much hope of persuading the Boche that the extensive preparations in the eastern Mediterranean were also directed at SICILY. For this reason they have told Wilson his cover plan should be something nearer the spot, e.g. the Dodecanese. Since our relations with Turkey are now so obviously closer the Italians must be pretty apprehensive about these islands.

I imagine you will agree with these arguments. I know you will have your hands more than full at the moment and you haven't much chance of discussing future operations with Eisenhower. But if by any chance you do want to support Wilson's proposal, I hope you will let us know soon, because we can't delay much longer.

I am very sorry we weren't able to meet your wishes about the new commander of the Guards Brigade. Your own nominee was down with a bad attack of 'flu and not likely to be really fit for another few weeks. No doubt, however, you know Forster personally; he has done extremely well in command of a brigade at home, and is, I think, the best fellow available.

You must be about as fed up as we are with the whole question of war medals and 'Purple Hearts.' We all agree with you that we don't want to offend our American friends, but there is a good deal more to it than that. If our troops who happen to be serving in one particular theatre are to get extra decorations merely because the Americans happen to be serving there too, we will be faced with a good deal of discontent among those troops fighting elsewhere perhaps just as bitterly—or more so. My own feeling is that we should thank the Americans for their kind offer, but say firmly it would cause too many anomalies and we are sorry we can't accept. But it is on the agenda for the next Military Members Meeting and I hope you will have a decision very soon.

Best of luck.

Yours ever,

ARCHIE NYE.

General the Hon. Sir Harold R. L. G. Alexander,
G.C.B., C.S.I., D.S.O., M.C.,
Headquarters,
18th Army Group.

Nothing could have been better; it carried out the scheme put up to him in a way that only someone who was himself fully in the picture of the personal relationships among high officers could have devised. Quite by inference, and so accidentally as to prevent the Germans thinking it a plant, it makes it clear that there will be an eastern Mediterranean operation with a landing in Greece, and it also makes it clear that we *want* the Germans to think that the western Mediterranean operation will be in Sicily (so *that* obviously *can't* be the real target); it does all that in an "off the record" atmosphere which, together with the very personal matters in the rest of the letter, makes it natural that it should not go through an official channel.

I had only two regrets. The first was that, knowing my Germans, I wanted to make certain that they had an absolutely definite target on which to fix as our western objective; but the Chiefs of Staff refused to sanction any mention of Sardinia in the letter; they thought that it would pinpoint Sicily too clearly if the Germans saw through our operation. However, after the Prime Minister's completely realistic appreciation of the situation, which I have already mentioned, I managed to get a joking reference to Sardinia inserted into another letter that we eventually drafted for Lord Louis Mountbatten to sign—and that, as will be seen, was of considerable value.

My second regret was less serious. I had wanted to include in the letter something which would appeal to the mind of the German reader as being consistent with thoughts that he already had. I felt that the average mind is readier to believe in the accuracy of a document if some part of it contains what he already knows. I had thought that the best way of getting an innocuous reference of this kind into the letter was to suggest a leg-pull of General Montgomery which might well coincide with the rather heavy-footed German humour. I therefore suggested that Sir Archibald should ask General Alexander, "What's gone wrong with Monty? He hasn't issued an Order of the Day for at least a week." Not long before this time General Montgomery had been issuing a number of Orders of the Day to encourage the troops, and a certain amount of ribaldry had resulted in various quarters. However, for some reason that I have never wholly fathomed, the Chiefs of Staff firmly banned my joke. I admit that it was a poor one, and its loss was not important, although I felt sure that the Germans would study and appreciate any joke of that kind.

Sir Archibald's letter was typed on his notepaper, addressed "My Dear Alex" and signed by him, and then enclosed and sealed in the usual double envelopes. The vital document was ready, and it was a pleasing touch that it happened to bear the date of St. George's Day.

5 Major Martin, Royal Marines

WHILE WE WERE PREPARING the document which we called the "vital letter" we had to consider the "man" who was going to carry it, for it was obvious that the first question that our opponent in Berlin would ask was: "How did the letter come to be at Huelva?" True, it was the sort of letter which would be carried by an officer, and not in an official bag; nevertheless, the German Intelligence officer would ask: "*Was* it carried by an officer? Did he seem to be a genuine officer?"

So we had to establish, as a first step, that the body was that of an officer. He had no uniform that we could use, as, for reasons both of security and of keeping my promise to conceal his identity, it was essential that we should provide him with a fresh uniform.

We had taken it for granted that, in his new personality, the body should be that of an army officer; this had, I think, followed in our minds from the fact that he was carrying a letter from the V.C.I.G.S. to the Commander-in-Chief of an army, and probably also from the fact that the wartime army was so large.

After a while, however, we decided against putting him in the army. There were a number of reasons for the decision, but the main and compelling one was concerned with the "distribution" of the signals and reports which would pass between the appropriate At-taché in Madrid and London after the body came ashore in Spain. Normally telegrams and signals were received in the appropriate office of the Service depart-ment concerned, and were then automatically distrib-uted to such officers and departments as might be interested in the subject to which they referred, the distribution being based on a series of distribution lists. As a result, any telegram which reported the finding of a dead body on the Spanish beach would be sent to the Service department concerned and would be automati-cally distributed to quite a number of people, and any follow-up telegrams would receive the same distribu-tion. Under the Admiralty system, it would be possible for me to arrange, with the authority of D.N.I., that this automatic distribution should be by-passed so that the messages resulting from our operation would be distributed to me only—and such an arrangement would not arouse comment. Under the War Office system, it was not easy to make any such arrangement for distribution to be limited either to me or to any col-league in the War Office.

So we decided that the body should not "join" the

army, but would have to come under the Admiralty—
and at once we found ourselves faced with a number of
problems that we had not visualised. He could not easily become a naval officer because, while an army officer could make such a flight as we were envisaging
from London to North African Headquarters wearing
a battledress, a naval officer would have had to wear
proper uniform—and although a battledress need not
fit too accurately, naval uniform would have to be made
to measure. We formed a horrid mental picture of
Gieves' cutter being brought down to measure and fit
our corpse for its uniform, and discarded that suggestion!

The only other possibility which would keep this
"officer" under naval control was that he should join
the Royal Marines: that would ease the problem of uniform, but it would bring a number of other problems.
Firstly, we had banked on the fact that the wartime
army was so big that there were many units whose officers would not be astonished if they heard of an officer
of their unit whom they did not know existed, whereas
the Royals are a small corps, and even in wartime
most of the officers know one another—or at least know
of one another. Secondly, there was the difficulty of ob-
taining a photograph. For various reasons, we had not
got, and could not get, any photograph of the young
man whose body we were using which was suitable for
an identity card in his new personality, and we had

banked on the fact that army officers did not carry
identity cards with photographs when going abroad—
but Royal Marine officers did.

We discussed these problems at some length; we
easily appreciated the danger that might be caused by
the small number that there was of Royal Marine officers, and that if the body *was* sent by the Spaniards to
Gibraltar for burial the danger that we had anticipated
if the body of an army officer was sent there would be
enormously increased; nevertheless, we decided that,
in view of the distance between Huelva and Gibraltar,
we could accept even the increased risk due to his being a Royal Marine. We decided also that we could
accept the difficulty of providing a suitable photograph,
but in this case we had not appreciated how great the
difficulty was.

First, we tried the expedient of taking photographs,
of the appropriate type, of the corpse; that was a complete failure. It is a common criticism of photographs
taken of living people for the subject to say, "Oh, it
makes me look as if I were dead!" Such criticism may
or may not be justified, but I defy anyone to take a
photograph of someone who *is* dead and to make it
look as if he could conceivably be alive: it is impossible
to describe how utterly and hopelessly dead any photograph of the body looked.

So a feverish search took place for a "double" of the
corpse—or even someone who resembled him sufficiently

Major Martin, Royal Marines

for a poor photo to give a reasonable appearance of what the owner of the body must have looked like in life. It was an odd thing, but although we had not thought that our young man had had an appearance which would have singled him out in a crowd, we could not find the man we wanted. All of us walked about for days staring rudely at anyone with whom we came in contact and who might, on some excuse, be persuaded to sit for his photo; eventually I decided to ask a young naval officer working in N.I.D.[1] to put on a battledress blouse and let us photograph him—I forget what excuse I used. The result, as I had anticipated, was not too good, but we decided that the likeness would suffice, bearing in mind the poor quality of such photographs.

And then we had another stroke of luck. Sitting opposite to me at a meeting to deal with quite a different matter, I saw someone who might have been the twin brother of the corpse; he was readily persuaded to let us photograph him, and that obstacle was surmounted.

The final step, before we could "commission" the body as an officer, was to give him a name and a rank. I felt that a very junior officer would be unlikely to be given such a letter as the vital document to carry, but we could not make him too senior for several reasons; the most important was that our body was too young to have achieved very high rank unless he had been so

[1] Naval Intelligence Division.

outstandingly able that his brother officers would be
bound to have heard of him. I therefore decided that
I would make him a captain (acting major); then I sat
down with a *Navy List;* I steadily went through the list
of Royal Marine officers until I found a little group of
about that same rank who all had the same name: that
name was "Martin."

There seemed to me to be an advantage in a group
of that kind. If the death of a "Major Martin" *did*
arouse discussion in a wardroom, there was always a
hope that those present would not know all the Martins
in the Royal Marines—or that, if they did, they would
think that there was an error in the initial given and
would not know whether to write and "condole." It
might not have worked out that way (indeed for all I
knew all the Martins were brothers), but this was only
an added precaution against a not too serious risk—and,
of course, there was bound to be some risk in any name
that I gave him. So I added the good normal Christian
name of "William," and our body became "Captain
(Acting Major) William Martin, Royal Marines," with
the approval of the Commandant-General, Royal
Marines, who agreed to accept him into that corps.
Finally, I laid on the necessary precautions in case any
enquiries were addressed to the C.G.R.M.'s department.

I had got a blank identity card and spent my time,
whenever seated, rubbing it up and down my trouser

Major Martin, Royal Marines

leg to try to produce the "patina" which such a document normally gets with time, even when carried in a wallet. I did not do so badly, but I was a little worried by the slow progress of the ageing process when I got another idea. I decided that Major Martin should have lost his original identity card and have had a new one issued. So I got a new blank, stuck in the photograph of Major Martin's double, filled in the particulars and signed it for him, and then got a suitable official to sign it as issued on the 2nd February 1943, "in lieu of No. 09650 lost"—the latter number being that of my own card, which would help to reduce complications if there were any subsequent enquiry—and got the appropriate stamps and seals put on it.

I had decided that Major Martin's "ship" should be Combined Operations H.Q., for reasons that I will deal with shortly, and chose Cardiff as his birthplace for no particular reason. The card being complete, I then proceeded to give it a reasonable degree of ageing by the trouser-rubbing process.

So the basis of Major Martin's personality was established; anyone finding his body could find *who* he was from his identity card. But I was sure that my German friends in Huelva, Madrid, or Berlin would want to know *why* Major Martin was going to North Africa: if we could let them find evidence answering that question it would increase faith in the "vital letter."

The Man Who Never Was

Why *should* a Royal Marine officer be flown out to North Africa? And why should he be flown out in such circumstances that the Vice-Chief of the Imperial General Staff would know of his going so that he could be entrusted with an important letter? Why?

After some thought, I found a reason which seemed plausible to our team. A seaborne operation was being mounted against a defended coast; this would involve the use of landing-craft, and it might well be that some hitch in training would call for assistance from an expert in that line; Major Martin could be that expert, and we decided to give him a document that made that clear.

I therefore drafted a letter for signature by Lord Louis Mountbatten, the Chief of Combined Operations, addressed to Admiral Sir Andrew Cunningham, Commander-in-Chief, Mediterranean. It was as follows:

> In reply quote: S.R. 1924/43
> Combined Operations Headquarters,
> 1A Richmond Terrace,
> Whitehall, S.W.1.
> 21st April, 1943.

DEAR ADMIRAL OF THE FLEET,

I promised V.C.I.G.S. that Major Martin would arrange with you for the onward transmission of a letter he has with him for General Alexander. It is very urgent and very "hot" and as there are some remarks in it that could not be seen by others in the War Office, it could not go by signal. I feel sure that you will see that it goes on safely and without delay.

I think you will find Martin the man you want. He is quiet and shy at first, but he really knows his stuff. He was more accurate than some of us about the probable run of events at Dieppe and he has been well in on the experiments with the latest barges and equipment which took place up in Scotland.

Let me have him back, please, as soon as the assault is over. He might bring some sardines with him—they are "on points" here!

Yours sincerely,
LOUIS MOUNTBATTEN.

Admiral of the Fleet Sir A. B. Cunningham,
G.C.B., D.S.O.,
Commander in Chief Mediterranean,
Allied Forces H.Q.,
Algiers.

I was rather pleased with that letter. It explained why Major Martin had the "vital letter" and why that had not been sent through official channels. It explained why Major Martin was being flown out. And, in view of the Prime Minister's clear realisation that it would not matter if Sicily was pinpointed by a failure of our operation, I was enabled to make a reference to Sardinia; I did this by a joke which was frightfully laboured, but I thought that that sort of joke would appeal to the Germans, who would be able to see the point and understand the reference. This joke, with its indication of Sardinia, was destined to play a part in our eventual success.

But there was yet one more ruse concealed in it. I was sure that the Germans in Berlin would get the "vital letter" or at least a copy of it, but I could not be sure that they would get more than a précis of what might be called the supporting documents, and I wanted to make certain that they would get this letter in full. I wanted Berlin to have the joke about Sardinia and I wanted them to have the explanation of why this officer was flying out and was carrying the unusual "vital document"; so I put in the bit about Dieppe. I was sure that no German could resist passing on to his superiors what he would feel to be an admission by the Chief of Combined Operations that our raid on Dieppe was not the success that we had hoped it would be. Whether or not I had accurately penetrated the German mind, this was the only one of Major Martin's documents, in addition to the vital document, of which we found a complete copy in the German files and which we know was studied in full by the German Intelligence in Berlin.

The letter was duly typed at Combined Operations H.Q. signed by Lord Louis, and given a fictitious, but plausible, reference number.

In the end we gave Major Martin one more letter to carry in addition to his personal papers. We were a little worried by the fact that an officer would prob-

Major Martin, Royal Marines

ably put two normal-sized envelopes into his pocket, or perhaps into his personal kit in spite of the secrecy of one of them. If Major Martin were to do this we had no absolute guarantee that the Spaniards would find them before handing over the body. We did not want to risk the German agent at Huelva having to curse his Spanish minions for not having searched the body. If only Major Martin could have an excuse for carrying the letters in a briefcase! We had to find him one.

It so happened that the official "pamphlet" on the Commandos by Hilary Saunders was about to be published in this country, and was to be accompanied by an American edition. We decided that it would be plausible for Lord Louis Mountbatten to have written a letter to General Eisenhower asking him for a Foreword for inclusion in the pamphlet. So a letter was drafted, making the request, and enclosing the proofs of that pamphlet and the photographs which it would contain, and we took the opportunity to include another little indication that Major Martin was a very responsible officer. This letter ran as follows:

> In reply quote: S.R. 1989/43.
> Combined Operations Headquarters,
> 1A Richmond Terrace,
> Whitehall, S.W.1.
> 22nd April, 1943.

DEAR GENERAL,

I am sending you herewith two copies of the pamphlet which has been prepared describing the activities of my

67

The Man Who Never Was

Command; I have also enclosed copies of the photographs which are to be included in the pamphlet.

The book has been written by Hilary St. George Saunders, the English author of *Battle of Britain, Bomber Command* and other pamphlets which have had a great success both in this country and yours.

The edition which is to be published in the States has already enjoyed pre-publication sales of nearly a million and a half and I understand the American authorities will distribute the book widely throughout the U.S. Army.

I understand from the British Information Service in Washington that they would like a "message" from you for use in the advertising for the pamphlet, and that they have asked you direct, through Washington, for such a message.

I am sending the proofs by hand of my Staff Officer, Major W. Martin of the Royal Marines. I need not say how honoured we shall all be if you will give such a message. I fully realise what a lot is being asked of you at a time when you are so fully occupied with infinitely more important matters. But I hope you may find a few minutes' time to provide the pamphlet with an expression of your invaluable approval so that it will be read widely and given every chance to bring its message of co-operation to our two peoples.

We are watching your splendid progress with admiration and pleasure and all wish we could be with you.

You may speak freely to Major Martin in this as well as any other matters since he has my entire confidence.

Yours sincerely,
LOUIS MOUNTBATTEN.

General Dwight Eisenhower,
Allied Forces H.Q., Algiers.

68

Major Martin, Royal Marines

This letter also was signed by Lord Louis and, when put into an envelope with its enclosures, it fully justified Major Martin in using a briefcase in which to carry all his official documents.

But our problem over this point did not end here. We had found an excuse for presenting the official documents to the Spaniards in a way that allowed for any inefficiency on their part and made sure that the documents would be discovered, but had we been too clever? Just as we were congratulating ourselves on our ingenuity, a sudden qualm arose: how on earth were we to ensure that the body and the briefcase arrived in Huelva together? Although it might be possible to place the handle of the briefcase into Major Martin's hand, we could not take the risk, on this all-important point, that the fingers might open and let the briefcase be dragged away by the sea. I made enquiries about *rigor mortis,* but, when I had added the complication that the body would have been frozen and then allowed to thaw, it was clear that the imponderables were far too many.

The only solution which we could devise was one which did not appeal to us, because it was the only point in the whole "set-up" which did not ring true. We decided to assume that an officer who carried really secret and important papers might attach his briefcase to one of the leather-covered chains which some bank-messengers use—wearing them down their sleeves so

69

they are not visible to the normal glance, but prevent their bag of valuables being snatched out of their hands. Such an arrangement seemed horribly phoney to us, but then *we* knew that this method was not one used by British officers. We decided that we would have to take a chance and rely on our opposite numbers in Berlin swallowing this feature. After all, *they* could not be sure that in no circumstances would a British officer adopt this method of safeguarding such documents.

So we decided to take the risk and use a chain. As may have been noted from the instructions to Lieutenant Jewell, we decided that Major Martin would not sit throughout a long flight with the briefcase dangling from his arm, and that it would be reasonable for him, instead of leaving this important bag to get lost or forgotten, to keep the bag on the chain, but to gain comfort by looping the latter through the belt of his trench-coat.

It is hard to be dogmatic: maybe we worried too much; maybe, on the other hand, the Germans in Berlin would have become suspicious over this point, had it been reported to them. I will not anticipate at this stage what we learned later, and will therefore only say that our luck was good and that question was never put to the test. Still, I would dearly like to know whether the risk that we took was a justifiable one, for we took it on the basis that the Spaniards would report accurately on this obviously important point, but that our opponents would not be sufficiently sure that the chain was a flaw in an otherwise convincing picture for them to take the risk of rejecting the genuineness of the documents. We will never know whether we were right or not. Perhaps it is just as well that we won't!

Finally, as Major Martin was serving at Combined Operations H.Q., he needed a special pass, and we got him one. We felt that we were in danger of making Major Martin into too great a paragon of all the virtues, and that it was about time that he should show some human failing in addition to the loss of his identity card. As will be seen, we were also engaged on building up a personal character for him which would reveal him as a little careless in his personal affairs, in spite of his ability as an officer, and we could not divorce his personal characteristics completely from his military ones. Besides (as is recounted in the next chapter), an event had taken place in his life which would be likely to drive such trivialities as the renewal of a pass from his mind. We therefore decided that he should make the same slip as most of us had done at one time or another, and forget to renew his pass. The one that we gave him expired on the 31st March 1943; we were sure that it would not surprise the Germans (any more than it would us) if Major Martin had been able to get away with the use of this pass until his departure in the third or fourth week of April.

It only remained to provide Major Martin with his uniform. One of us who happened to have approximately the same build as Major Martin got a suitable battledress, to which we added Royal Marine and Commando flashes and a major's crown. An old trench-coat was obtained, and we put similar badges of rank on the shoulder straps after having pierced them for the three "pips" of his substantive rank. Boots and webbing gaiters were got in addition to a shirt and all his underwear; these last were not new, but all old laundry-marks were removed from them and his hand-kerchiefs, and they were then all laundered together so as finally to have the same marks.

We had bought a shirt at Gieves, and we thought that Bill Martin might well have stuffed the scrumpled bill into the pocket of his trench-coat. This produced the only real brick which we dropped: the officer who actually bought the shirt was not in the Navy, and he took the unbelievable step of paying cash. As Bill Martin hadn't an account there it would have been difficult for the officer to do otherwise without getting the wrong name on the bill, but, after the body was out of our reach, I suddenly realised that few naval officers had ever been known to pay cash to Gieves, least of all one who was being dunned for his overdraft! I could, however, comfort myself with the thought that it was the *Germans* that we had to deceive; *they* could not know for certain whether temporary officers were still granted the same privileges by that long-suffering firm as were given to the Regulars. Still —it was a mistake and inartistic.

So the body of the "man who never was" had become that of an officer, Major Martin of the Royal Marines, and anyone who found the body would have ample evidence of who he was and why he was where he was. But it was still the body of an officer and not that of a person. We had still to provide him with his personal effects and with a human personality to make him "real."

6 The Creation of a Person

FROM QUITE an early stage Major Martin had become a real person to us and it was obviously desirable that as much of that feeling as possible should be shared by whoever investigated the body; the more real he appeared the more convincing the whole affair would be. Besides, I was quite sure that in a matter of this importance every little detail would be studied by the Germans in an effort to find a flaw in Major Martin's make-up, so as to be sure that the whole thing was genuine and not a plant. That I was not mistaken is evidenced by the fact that, as we learnt later, the Germans even noticed the dates on the two theatre-ticket stubs that we placed in Major Martin's pocket.

The method that we adopted in deciding on Major Martin's personality was to keep on discussing him—rather as if we were pulling a friend to pieces behind his back. In fact, we talked about him until we did feel that he was an old friend whom we had known for years. I must, however, admit that, although he

74

became completely real to us, we did tend to mould his character and history to suit our convenience.

As I have just related, we had decided that Major Martin was a rather brilliant officer and was trusted by his superiors: his only visible lapses were the all too common ones of having lost his identity card and having recently let his pass to Combined Operations H.Q. run out of date.

On that foundation we built a character which could be evidenced by documents in his pockets: that was the only means that we had whereby to convey his personality to the Germans.

We decided that he should be fond of a good time, so he could have an invitation to a night club; it was a probable result of a certain amount of extravagance that he would have a letter from his bank about his overdraft; he could have been staying at a Service club while in London, so he might have a receipted bill for the last part of his stay there. In this way he was developing from an abstraction into something rather more definite.

But how could we make him really "come to life"?

The only way to do it was by letting him carry in his pockets letters which would convey to the reader something really personal about him. On the other hand, if one were able to stop a passer-by in the street and search his pockets, it would be very seldom that one would hit on any occasion when he had letters about him which covered more than trivial details. When we approached our problem in that way, we came to the conclusion that the only times when a man is certain to be carrying "live" letters conveying a vivid picture of him and his life would be when he had recently become engaged and was carrying love letters on him and making arrangements for married life. We therefore decided that "a marriage should be arranged" between Bill Martin and some girl just before he was sent abroad.

So Major Martin "met" a charming girl called Pam early in April, became engaged to her almost at once (those wartime courtships!); she gave him a snap of herself and he gave her an engagement ring; he had a couple of ecstatic letters from her, one written when staying away the week-end and one written in the office (while her boss was out) in an agony of emotion, as he had hinted that he was being sent abroad somewhere. He would have with him the bill for the engagement ring—unpaid of course, as he had an overdraft to deal with. Lastly, he could have an old-fashioned father who disapproved of war weddings and who would insist on his son making a will if he persisted in so foolish and improvident a step.

We felt that we could not hope to build up a personality more definitely than that with only a pocketful of letters—but they had to sound genuine and they had to be written by someone. We could, of course, have written them ourselves—most of us knew only too well what a letter about an overdraft looked like, and some of us had made wills or received love letters, but I thought it best to rely on the expert hand so that there could be no possibility of any mistake.

Some of the items were easy. For instance, one of our number had an invitation to the Cabaret Club with no name on it, so the night club was easily provided for. The letter about the overdraft was only slightly more difficult. Through another of our number we got a letter from Lloyds Bank dated the 14th April calling on Major Martin to pay off an overdraft of some £79. I was asked, later on, whether it was usual for a letter dealing with such a comparatively small sum to have been signed by the Joint General Manager at Head Office; I had already considered this, as I know from bitter experience that such letters are usually signed by the branch manager. When I raised this question at the time, I was assured that, although it was true that such letters were more usually signed by the manager of the appropriate branch, it did quite often happen that the letter would come from Head Office in certain circumstances. As the officer concerned in getting this letter had a "lead in" to the Head Office, it was decided to use that: I did not think that the Germans would have had the experience that we had had of overdrafts and, after all, even if the amount was small, Major Martin's father was clearly a man of some importance. This letter was drafted for us personally by Mr. Whitley Jones, the Joint General Manager of Lloyds Bank, typed in his office and signed by him. It read as follows:

Lloyds Bank Limited
Head Office
London, E.C.3.

Private   14th April, 1943.

Major W. Martin, R.M.,

Army and Navy Club,
Pall Mall,
London, S.W.1.

DEAR SIR,

I am given to understand that in spite of repeated application your overdraft amounting to £79. 19s. 2d. still outstands.

In the circumstances, I am now writing to inform you that unless this amount, plus interest at 4% to date of payment, is received forthwith we shall have no alternative but to take the necessary steps to protect our interests.

Yours faithfully,
(*Signed*) E. WHITLEY JONES,
Joint General Manager.

It had been arranged that this letter from the bank should be sent through the post to Major Martin at the Naval and Military Club, but it was erroneously posted addressed to him at the Army and Navy Club, Pall Mall; there the Hall Porter marked the envelope "Not known at this address" and added "Try Naval and

The Creation of a Person

Military Club, 94 Piccadilly." This seemed to us to be a most convincing indication that the letter was real and not specially prepared, so we decided that Major Martin should keep this letter in its envelope.

One of us had got the co-operation of the Naval and Military Club; we had been given a bill dated the 24th April which showed that Major Martin had been a temporary member of that club and had stayed there for the nights of the 18th to 23rd April inclusive; apart from its other purpose of general build-up of the Major's personality, it afforded a strong indication that he was still in London on the 24th.

Similarly, there was but little difficulty in getting the bill for the engagement ring. I chose S. J. Phillips, the Bond Street jewellers, as I knew that they had an international trade, so that it was probable that there would be bill-heads of theirs available in Germany to prove, if comparison were to be made, how genuine Major Martin's bill was. That bill was dated the 19th April, but showed that the ring had actually been bought on the 15th.

We were in some difficulty in getting these and the other documents. Obviously, the true story of why we wanted them could not be told, but I was convinced that just to ask for them and to give no reason, except that it was for something secret, was liable to cause talk; on the other hand, once a plausible reason was given we felt sure that we could rely on those whom we approached.

So my "cover story" was that there was someone who seemed suspiciously interested in officers who were temporarily hard up: we wanted to have some documents, building up towards a shortage of money, which a particular person could leave about his rooms where they would be seen by this individual. We could then observe what his conduct was. This seemed to be a satisfying story, and we received ready help—and no one ever let us down with the slightest leak.

What might be called the supporting cast among the documents having been provided for, we now had to obtain the "stars."

First of all we needed a suitable snapshot of Pam, Major Martin's fiancée. The scheme which we devised was to ask the more attractive girls in our various offices to lend us a snapshot of themselves for use in a photographic identity parade—the sort of thing where the photographs of one or two suspects are shuffled in among those of a number of perfectly innocent persons and the "witness" is asked to pick out the one of the person whom he had seen; we asked for a variegated lot, and got quite a collection. We eventually chose a charming photograph and returned the remainder. The subject of the photograph was working in the War Office and, as she had access to "Top Secret" papers, we were able to tell her that we wanted to use the photograph

The Creation of a Person

as that of someone's fictitious fiancée in a deception, and she gave her permission.

None of us had felt up to writing the love letters—after all, ours was not the feminine point of view—and it was a bit difficult to ask a girl whether she could write a first-rate pæan of love. So we asked a girl working in one of the offices whether she could get some girl to do it. She took on the job, but never would tell us the name of the girl who produced the two magnificent letters that Major Martin was to carry with him.

I had decided that the first of these should be written on my brother-in-law's notepaper, for I was sure that no German could resist the "Englishness" of such an address as "The Manor House, Ogbourne St. George, Marlborough, Wiltshire"; this letter, dated "Sunday 18th," ran as follows:

The Manor House,
Ogbourne St. George,
Marlborough, Wiltshire.
Telephone: Ogbourne St. George 242.
Sunday, 18th.

I do think dearest that seeing people like you off at railway stations is one of the poorer forms of sport. A train going out can leave a howling great gap in ones life & one has to try madly—& quite in vain—to fill it with all the things one used to enjoy a whole five weeks ago. That lovely golden day we spent together—oh! I know it has been said before, but if *only* time could sometimes stand still just for a *minute*—But that line of thought is too pointless. Pull your socks up Pam & dont be a silly little fool.

Your letter made me feel slightly better—but I shall get horribly conceited if you go on saying things like that about me—they're utterly unlike ME, as I'm afraid you'll soon find out. Here I am for the weekend in this divine place with Mummy & Jane being too sweet & understanding the whole time, bored beyond words & panting for Monday so that I can get back to the old grindstone again. What an idiotic waste!

Bill darling, do let me know as soon as you get fixed & can make some more plans, & dont *please* let them send you off into the blue the horrible way they do nowadays—now that we've found each other out of the whole world, I dont think I could bear it—

All my love,

PAM.

It was followed by two sheets of plain paper, such as was used in Government offices for carbon copies; the letter was headed "Office, Wednesday, 21st," and the writing, which started reasonably good, suddenly degenerated into a scrawl as the letter was hastily brought to an end when the writer's boss was heard returning. It ran:

Office.

Wednesday, 21st.

The Bloodhound has left his kennel for half an hour so here I am scribbling nonsense to you again. Your letter came this morning just as I was dashing out—madly late as usual! You do write such heavenly ones. But what are these

The Creation of a Person

horrible dark hints you're throwing out about being sent off somewhere—*of course* I won't say a word to anyone—I never do when you tell me things, but it's not abroad is it? Because I won't have it, I won'T, tell them so from me. Darling, why did we go and meet in the middle of a war, such a silly thing for anybody to do—if it weren't for the war we might have been nearly married by now, going round together choosing curtains etc. And I wouldn't be sitting in a dreary Government office typing idiotic minutes all day long —I *know* the futile sort of work I do doesn't make the war one minute shorter—

Dearest Bill, I'm so thrilled with my ring—scandalously extravagant—you know how I adore diamonds—I simply can't stop looking at it.

I'm going to a rather dreary dance tonight with Jock & Hazel, I think they've got some other man coming. You know what their friends always turn out to be like, he'll have the sweetest little Adam's apple & the shiniest bald head! How beastly & ungrateful of me, but it isn't really that—you know—don't you?

Look darling, I've got next Sunday & Monday off for Easter. I shall go home for it of course, *do* come too if you possibly can, or even if you can't get away from London I'll dash up and we'll have an evening of gaiety—(By the way Aunt Marian said to bring you to dinner next time I was up, but I think that might wait?)

Here comes the Bloodhound, masses of love & a kiss

from

PAM.

We felt that we had been well served, and that the letters were ideal for our purpose.

The Man Who Never Was

To take the part of Major Martin's father we chose a young wartime officer who produced a brilliant tour de force; the letter of the 13th April and the enclosure seemed to me to be so redolent of Edwardian pomposity that no one *could* have invented them—no one but a father of the old school could have written them. The letter and its enclosure read:

Tel. No. 98.

Black Lion Hotel,
Mold,
N. Wales.
13th April, 1943.

MY DEAR WILLIAM,

I cannot say that this Hotel is any longer as comfortable as I remember it to have been in pre war days. I am, however, staying here as the only alternative to imposing myself once more upon your aunt whose depleted staff & strict regard for fuel economy (which I agree to be necessary in war time) has made the house almost uninhabitable to a guest, at least one of my age. I propose to be in Town for the nights of the 20th & 21st of April when no doubt we shall have an opportunity to meet. I enclose the copy of a letter which I have written to Gwatkin of McKenna's about your affairs. You will see that I have asked him to lunch with me at the Carlton Grill (which I understand still to be open) at a quarter to one on Wednesday the 21st. I should be glad if you would make it possible to join us. We shall not however wait luncheon for you, so I trust that, if you are able to come, you will make a point of being punctual.

Your cousin Priscilla has asked to be remembered to you.

The Creation of a Person

She has grown into a sensible girl though I cannot say that her work for the Land Army has done much to improve her looks. In that respect I am afraid that she will take after her father's side of the family.

Your affectionate

FATHER.

Copy
Tel. No. 98.

Black Lion Hotel,

Mold,

N. Wales.

10th April.

MY DEAR GWATKIN,

I have considered your recent letter concerning the Settlement which I intend to make on the occasion of William's marriage. The provisions which you outline appear to me reasonable except in one particular. Since in this case the wife's family will not be contributing to the settlement I do not think it proper that they should necessarily preserve, after William's death, a life interest in the funds which I am providing. I should agree to this course only were there children of the marriage. Will you therefore so redraft the Settlement as to provide that if there are children the income is paid to the wife only until such time as she remarries or the children come of age. After that date the children alone should benefit.

I intend to be in London for the two nights of the 20th & 21st of April. I should be glad if you could make it convenient to take luncheon with me at the Carlton Grill at a quarter to one on Wednesday 21st. If you will bring the new draft with you we shall have leisure to examine it afterwards. I have written to William & hope that he will be able to join us.

Yrs. sincerely,

(*Signed*) J. G. MARTIN.

F. A. S. Gwatkin, Esq.,
McKenna & Co.,
14 Waterloo Place,
London, S.W.1.

We selected the Black Lion Hotel, Mold, not only because it also seemed so British an address that it in itself conveyed an impression of truth, but it was also consistent with Major Martin's birthplace of Cardiff; I hope that they will forgive us for taking and using their notepaper—and especially for questioning the comfort for which that hotel is noted.

Finally, I got a friend who was a partner in the firm to round off the picture by drafting the following letter, and writing it on McKenna & Co.'s note-paper:

McKenna & Co.   14, Waterloo Place,
Solicitors.   London, S.W.1.

Our ref.: McL/EG

19th April, 1943.

DEAR SIR,

Re your affairs

We thank you for your letter of yesterday's date returning the draft of your will approved. We will insert the legacy of £50 to your batman and our Mr. Gwatkin will bring the fair copy with him when he meets you at lunch on the 21st inst. so that you can sign it there.

The Creation of a Person

The inspector of taxes has asked us for particulars of your service pay and allowances during 1941/2 before he will finally agree to the amount of reliefs due to you for that year. We cannot find that we have ever had these particulars and shall, therefore, be grateful if you will let us have them.

Yours faithfully,
McKenna & Co.

Major W. Martin, R.M.,
Naval & Military Club,
94, Piccadilly,
London, W.1.

When we read all those documents together they conveyed to us the impression of a real person—of a real person who lived—of a man who really was. We did not feel that more could be done with the few papers that a man could reasonably have in his pocket.

However, we took some precautions before we gave the letters to Major Martin. The letters, other than the love letters, I carried in my pockets for the appropriate number of days to get them into the right condition. But the love letters were more of a problem, especially as one of them was on flimsy paper. It was obvious that they would have been read and re-read and would not be in mint condition, but the proper appearance could not be produced quickly by scrumpling them up and then smoothing them out again (as someone foolishly suggested would be the suitable method); once a piece of paper has been scrumpled no amount of flattening will erase the fact that it has been treated that way—and the one thing that Bill Martin would never have done to those letters was to crush them up. So I did what he would have done; I folded and unfolded the letters again and again, and in addition I rubbed them carefully on my clothing to get a little patina on to them.

1. Major Martin sets out

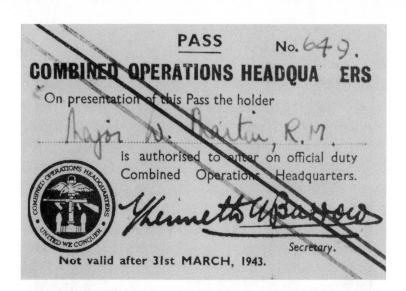

PASS   No. 649.

COMBINED OPERATIONS HEADQUARTERS

On presentation of this Pass the holder

Major W. Martin, R.M.

is authorised to enter on official duty
Combined   Operations   Headquarters.

Kenneth M. Barrow

Secretary.

Not valid after 31st MARCH, 1943.

Pass is not transferable. If found, it should
be handed in at any Police Station, or sent to—

The Secretary,
Combined Operations Headquarters,
IA Richmond Terrace,
Whitehall, S.W.I.

Signature of holder   _W. Martin_

(C.6465)

2. Major Martin's pass to Combined Operations Headquarters

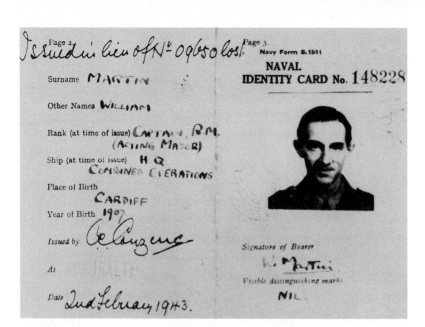

3. Identity card

4. Theatre tickets

COMBINED OPERATIONS HEADQUARTERS,
1A, RICHMOND TERRACE,
WHITEHALL, S.W.1.

Telephone
Whitehall 9777

21st April,
1 9 4 3.

Dear Admiral of the Fleet,

    I promised V.C.I.G.S. that Major Martin would
arrange with you for the onward transmission of a
letter he has with him for General Alexander. It is
very urgent and very "hot" and as there are some
remarks in it that could not be seen by others in the
War Office, it could not go by signal. I feel sure
that you will see that it goes on safely and without
delay.

    I think you will find Martin the man you want.
He is quiet and shy at first, but he really knows his
stuff. He was more accurate than some of us about the
probable run of events at Dieppe and he has been well
in on the experiments with the latest barges and
equipment which took place up in Scotland.

    Let me have him back, please, as soon as the
assault is over. He might bring some sardines with him -
they are "on points" here!

Yours sincerely,

Louis Mountbatten

Admiral of the Fleet Sir A.B. Cunningham, G.C.B., D.S.O.,
Commander in Chief Mediterranean,
Allied Force H.Q.,
Algiers.

5. Letter from Lord Louis Mountbatten to Admiral Cunningham

6. Some of the 'corroborative details'

Office
Thursday 21st

The Bloodhound has left his kennel for half an hour so here I am scribbling nonsense to you again. Your letter came this morning just as I was dashing out — madly late as usual! You do write such heavenly ones. But what are these portents dark hints you're throwing out about being sent off somewhere? Of course I won't say a word to anyone — I never do when you tell me things — but it's not abroad is it? Because I won't have it I won't. Tell them so from me. Darling, why did we go & marry in the middle of a war, such a silly

Here comes the Bloodhound, masses of love & a kiss from

7. The Blood-hound goes—and comes back

8. Pam

TELEPHONE Nº MAYfair 6261 (2 LINES)
TELEGRAMS EUCLASE WESDO LONDON.

113 New Bond Street

London W.1. 19ᵗʰ April 1943.

Major W. Martin R.M.,
   Naval + Military Club,
   94 Piccadilly . W.1.

To S. J. Phillips.
Silversmith.
Jewels, Antique Plate, Bijouterie.

April. 1943.   Single diamond ring small dia⁀
              shoulders plat⁀ (pre purchase tax)   52 10 -

              Engraving "P.L. from W.M. 14.4.43" p   10 6

                                                 £ 53 - 6

9. The bill for the engagement ring

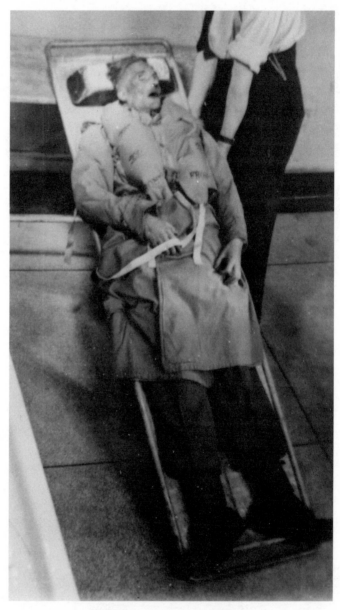

10. Major Martin goes to war

7 Major Martin
Gets Ready for War

WE HAD GONE steadily on with our preparations although final approval for the launching of the operation had not yet been obtained.

After considering Sir Archibald Nye's letter, the Chiefs of Staff had given approval in principle; we now pressed for authority to start. There was bound to be a conflict of interest at this stage: the Chiefs of Staff were naturally reluctant to become committed to the Germans receiving the information contained in the letter as our strategy *might* be changed—if that had happened it would not have been for the first time! On the other hand, we simply *had* to get the letter to Spain by the beginning of May if the operation was to be of any value; we had to give the German Intelligence Service time to get the information, convince themselves of its genuineness by any check-up that they might want, and then to "appreciate" it and pass the result on to the Operational Staff. The latter would then need time to make their arrangements and to send their forces to the wrong places—and, if we wanted them not to fortify Sicily, it was no good waiting until those fortifications were complete.

The Chiefs of Staff accepted this necessity and gave their final approval, subject to reference to the Prime Minister, to whom the matter was submitted through General Ismay.

When the Prime Minister was told that there was some risk of pinpointing Sicily, if the operation went wrong, he replied (as I have already recorded), "I don't see that that matters. Anybody but a damn' fool would *know* it is Sicily." We felt that he ought also to be informed that our efforts might be wasted, as there was always the chance that the body *might* be recovered by a Spaniard who was not co-operating with the Germans and the papers might be returned to us intact. The Prime Minister realised that that risk was not great either, and disposed of this point with a grin and a chuckle, saying, "I don't see that that matters either. We can always try again"!

So we had received the all-clear, subject to General Eisenhower being informed of the plan. If he had had any objection, or any change of strategy had occurred before the body was actually launched, the operation could have been cancelled in the way I had provided in paragraph 8 of the "operation orders" to Lieutenant Jewell.

Major Martin Gets Ready for War

Meanwhile we had to undertake the least pleasant part of our work—we had to get the body ready for its mission.

We heartily disliked this task. In spite of the great service which we were confident that the body would render to its country, it went against the grain to disturb its rest; in addition, there was an odd psychological reaction on each occasion that we saw the body lying stiff and cold. By this time Major Martin had become a completely living person for us; we felt that we knew him just as one knows one's best friend. After all, one has to be very close to a friend to read his love letters and the very personal letters that he gets from his father; we had come to feel that we had known Bill Martin from his early childhood and were taking a genuine and personal interest in the progress of his courtship and financial troubles. I had thought that I might say that we, who had created him, knew him as a father knows his son—but that would have been inaccurate. We knew him far better than most fathers know their sons; so as to create him we had had to make ourselves know his every thought and his probable reaction to any event that might occur in his life.

So we never relished the prospect of a visit to the place where the corpse was in cold storage—and George and I had to pay no less than three visits to him. First we had to disturb him to try to get a suitable photograph, and we took that opportunity to check his measurements, and especially the size that he took in boots. Then we thought it wise to pay a second visit and dress him so that he was fully ready for his journey in case there was any hitch which could not be rectified in haste. And it was a good thing that we did, for we had forgotten one point.

I have used the expression "lying stiff and cold." We had realized that it would be difficult to dress a body fully, from the underwear up, when it was in such a condition; we had checked on the situation when we took the photographs and found that, although difficult, it was possible. But we had forgotten the boots!

To appreciate what we were up against, it would be necessary for you to try to put a pair of boots on your feet, keeping your ankle and foot absolutely rigid, and with the latter at right angles to the leg—the operation is utterly impossible.

This was a bad check: we knew that to freeze and then to thaw a body, and then to freeze it again is a sure way to hasten the process of decomposition when eventually the body is allowed finally to thaw out. If we had to do this we might well vitiate the whole basis of Sir Bernard Spilsbury's calculations. What were we to do?

Suddenly we thought of the solution. We got an electric fire and thawed the feet and ankles only; then hurriedly, yet carefully, we dressed the body completely, and finally, with sincere mental apologies for

Major Martin Gets Ready for War

what we were doing to it, replaced it in the cold storage.

Our third visit was on Saturday the 17th April, 1943 at 6 p.m., when we went to fetch Major Martin for the start of his journey. First we put the personal letters and the wallet with his passes and so on into his pockets. Then we added the usual "junk" that a man carries about on him, or unwittingly collects in his pockets. The final list was somewhat impressive:

Identity discs (2) "Major W. MARTIN, R.M., R/C," attached to braces.
Silver cross on silver chain round neck.
Watch, wrist.
Wallet, containing:
    Photograph of fiancée.
    Book of stamps (2 used).
    2 letters from fiancée.
    St. Christopher plaque.
    Invitation to Cabaret Club.
    C.C.O. Pass ⎫ in cellophane
    Admiralty Identity Card ⎰ container.
    Torn-off top of letter.
    1 £5 note—5th March, 1942 $\frac{227}{C}$ 45827.
    3 £1 notes X34D527008
                W21D029293
                X66D443119
1 half-crown.
2 shillings.
2 sixpences.

The Man Who Never Was

4 pennies.

Letter from "Father."

Letter from "Father" to McKenna & Co., solicitors.

Letter from Lloyds Bank.

Bill (receipted) from Naval and Military Club.

Bill (cash) from Gieves Ltd.

Bill for engagement ring.

2 bus tickets.

2 counterfoil stubs of tickets for Prince of Wales' Theatre, 22nd April, 1943.

Box of matches.

Packet of cigarettes.

Bunch of keys.

Pencil stub.

Letter from McKenna & Co., solicitors.

I must digress here to explain the item "2 counterfoil stubs of tickets for Prince of Wales' Theatre, 22nd April, 1943." As I have said, it was on the 17th April that we went to fetch Major Martin, and he was to sail on the 19th; he was due to be launched into the sea off Huelva on about the 29th or 30th April. On the other hand, if he had been travelling by air, as we wanted the Germans to believe, the journey would only have taken a single day. When we considered this difference in time, we decided to work the time-table back the other way: if we deducted from the arrival in Huelva on about the 30th April some five or six days in which the body might have been drifting ashore from an aircraft which had come to grief out at sea (we had reckoned that the eventual degree of decomposition would probably support an immersion of about that period), that would mean that Major Martin would have left London on about the 24th of April, and for that reason the bill for his room at the Naval and Military Club was dated that day. But here George had another of his brilliant ideas; it suddenly came into his ingenious mind that anyone who sees the stub of a theatre ticket at once assumes that the ticket has been used, but there was no reason why we should not buy theatre tickets valid for any date after the body had in fact left London, and then tear off the stubs and waste the tickets. So we decided that Bill Martin and Pam should have a farewell party before he left; we felt that they would enjoy the Sid Fields show at the Prince of Wales' Theatre, and we bought four tickets for that show (the reason why we bought four will be related later), tore off the stubs of two and put them into Major Martin's pocket. Once again a small detail was to play its part in the deception, and this afterthought "went home" whereas the bill for the room at the Club was overlooked by the Spaniards and Germans.

Finally, we added the briefcase containing the important documents, and here we made a slight alteration from our intended arrangements of which I had notified Lieutenant Jewell. We had intended to take the briefcase up to the Clyde separately from the canister and give it into Lieutenant Jewell's care, but when it came to the point we found that the bag could be inserted into the canister with the body; and we therefore took this course, as it was an obvious safeguard against any forgetfulness during the launching of the body off Huelva. Lieutenant Jewell would have a difficult task, especially if it was rough, and his mind would be fully occupied with that and the safety of his ship: it would have been a pity if Major Martin had floated ashore while his briefcase remained in Lieutenant Jewell's safe.

When we had completed the clothing, filled all the pockets and attached the briefcase, we wrapped the body in a blanket so as to prevent it getting rubbed during its journey. When we had arrived we had stood the canister up on end and filled it with dry ice; when this had melted, we refilled the canister and again waited for the ice to melt. Then we lifted Major Martin and reverently and carefully lowered him into the canister and packed him round with still more dry ice. Finally, we put on the lid and screwed down the nuts. Major Martin was ready to go to war.

8 The Journey North

Our party consisted of George and myself, together with Jock Horsfall, the racing motorist, who was on special duty with the War Office, one of whose 30-cwt. Ford vans we had borrowed—and, of course, Major Martin in his canister.

The journey nearly ended almost before it had started for, as we drove out from the "cold storage" to start back to George's flat in London, we caught sight of a queue waiting to see a spy film at the local cinema; the same thought flashed into each of our minds: what would those people think if we were to stop and say to them, "Don't bother about the film. We can tell you a much better story—and ours is true. Just look inside this canister"? And we all burst out laughing to such an extent that Jock almost rammed a tram-standard.

But we got safely back to George's flat. There we cooked ourselves some dinner and ate it, taking turns to keep an eye on the van outside; if a thief had got away with the canister, he would have had a disap-

97

pointment—and a shock—when he opened it, but his disappointment would have been nothing to ours. So we made ourselves some sandwiches and filled thermos flasks as we realized that we could not leave the van during the journey north.

Our preparations completed, we set off for Greenock, Jock and I taking it in turns to drive. It was a long and tiring journey, as we could, of course, only use masked headlights; at one point we drove straight across a "roundabout" which, fortunately, only had smooth grass in its centre once we had mounted the kerb. The sound of aircraft overhead added to our worries; for although the *Seraph* was not due to sail until the 19th and we had got a fair amount of time in hand in which to cope, without any really serious consequences, with any traffic diversions through bomb damage, Lieutenant Jewell had asked that we should arrive before midday on the 18th, in case there were any last-minute difficulties in stowing the canister. However, we did not crash the van and, as far as I know, all the aircraft were friendly, so we drove on through the night, taking it in turns to sleep on the floor of the van.

Early on the morning of the 18th we arrived at Greenock and drove to the dock, where we had arranged to meet the launch that was to ferry us out to H.M.S. *Forth*, the submarine depot ship lying in the Holy Loch.

The Journey North

Here we ran up against a snag. I had visualised that there might be some difficulty in lowering the canister into the launch, so I had carefully said in the signal from D.N.I. arranging for our arrival that I would have "one, repeat one" package weighing over 400 lb. and requesting assistance in embarking it. In spite of that particularity, the signal had been read as if our total baggage weighed 400 lb. in several packages. As a result, we found ourselves faced with a launch surging up and down some feet below the quay and the "party" for which we had asked consisted of one rating. He was very obliging, but no rope was available and to lower the canister without disaster was clearly impossible.

Anticipating all sorts of trouble and delay before I, a complete stranger, could arrange for a party to be got together, I hurried off to the Flag Officer in Charge's headquarters—and my luck still held. The Duty Officer on duty turned out to be a Wren who had been serving as a rating in the signal office at Hull when I was on the Staff there. We greeted one another as old friends and, all difficulties having been quickly smoothed out, I returned to the dock with half a dozen ratings and some rope with which to lower the canister.

We were soon ferried down to H.M.S. *Forth*, where I handed Major Martin over to Lieutenant Jewell. I also gave him the rubber dinghy which he was to launch with the body; so as to give the impression of an accident and haste, the dinghy was to be launched upside down, and it seemed better to leave only one of the collapsible aluminium oars in it; I therefore kept the other one, and I still have it as a souvenir. As it turned out, however, the launching of the dinghy made no difference; a body might be of no value to a Spanish fisherman, but a rubber dinghy certainly was—so ours was never heard of again. I hope the finder made good use of it.

We had been advised that, if a Catalina flying boat sank out at sea, it was unlikely that any wreckage would float ashore, so we did not provide Lieutenant Jewell with anything more with which to simulate signs of a disaster.

The canister was duly stowed on board H.M.S. *Seraph* and I had final discussions with Lieutenant Jewell. In these I suggested that he might be able to launch the body with only officers present on deck. If he could, it would reduce the number of persons who were "in the know" and thus make leakage of the story less likely—and it was more than usually important to guard against leakage, as the story of the launching of a dead body off the coast of Spain was one that would tempt the best of us to gossip.

If he could launch the body in this way, he would obviously need a "cover story" for the rest of the crew, who would see a package that they had thought to be destined for Malta taken up on deck off the coast of

Spain, after which it would never reappear. I suggested that he might tell them that the so-called optical instruments were, in fact, a secret weather-reporting buoy and that, if the Spaniards learned of its existence, they would remove it. If he had to have the crew on deck during the launching, either because of rough weather or for any other reason, he would use the cover story that I had given him in the "operation orders."

All went well with our arrangements, and on our return to London we were able to end our report with the statement: "On April 19th, 1943 at 1800 British Double Summer Time H.M. s/m *Seraph* sailed from Holy Loch." Remembering the nature of the cargo, I felt that these names were most suitable and augured well for the success of the operation.

9 The Launching
of the Body

THERE THEN CAME a period of anxiety; I had never had
any qualms about the success of the operation, but now
that its execution was out of my hands I kept thinking
of things that might go wrong. Oddly enough, I still
did not worry whether the Germans would see through
the deception. I was confident that they would not. My
anxiety was confined to the launching of the body.
Could we really be sure that the body would float
ashore or would I have to confess, after all the effort,
that the whole thing was a complete flop? And, in my
worst moments, I visualised the *Seraph* getting into
trouble off Huelva, where she had gone only because
of my plan. Still, I had more than enough to do with
my other duties not to have much time for worry, and
we did have at least one very cheerful evening during
this period.

It had seemed absurd to waste the tickets, the stubs
of which Major Martin had in his pocket. So we had,
as I have recorded, bought four tickets, and we took

The Launching of the Body

care to give Major Martin the stubs of the middle two seats of the four.

George and I then invited "Pam" and Jill, the girl who had arranged for the writing of the love letters, to "Bill Martin's farewell party." We started at the Prince of Wales' Theatre, where the manager let us in after he had inspected the block of tickets and we had explained that someone had torn the stubs off the centre pair "as a joke"—we did not tell him that the joke was on the Germans.

After the theatre we went on to the Gargoyle Club for dinner. There we were shown to one of the side tables which had a banquette faced by two chairs. I suggested that the two girls should take the more comfortable banquette, but Jill turned to George and said, "Considering Bill and Pam are engaged, they are the least affectionate couple I know. They don't even want to sit together at his farewell party before he goes abroad." At this the couple at the next table looked round and pricked up their ears.

I "explained" to Jill that even if Pam and I were engaged we had only known one another for a few days (obvious disapproval of war weddings registered at the next table), and then added, as an afterthought, that it would be different when Pam and I knew one another better, for my boss had said (in the letter that she had seen [1]) that, although I was quiet and shy at

[1] Lord Louis Mountbatten's letter to Admiral Cunningham.

first, I really did know my stuff. At this the couple at the next table registered even stronger disapproval and got up and danced.

I might interpolate another result of this joking identification of Bill Martin with me. Pam followed it up by giving me a larger copy of the photograph that was on its way to Spain in Bill Martin's wallet, and signed it "Till death do us part. Your loving Pam"—a safe inscription, as "I" was already "dead." At that time I was staying with my mother, and to see her reaction I put the photograph on my dressing table. I was disappointed—she said nothing. About a year later, when my wife returned from America, where she had been doing a job in our Security Co-ordination Service, I showed her the photograph, and she astonished me by saying, "So *that* was why your mother started writing in her letters that she felt that I should come home as soon as my job allowed it"!

While we were waiting in London, the *Seraph* was having an uneventful passage to the coast of Spain. The first news that we got was from the pre-arranged signal which informed us, on the 30th April, that "Operation Mincemeat" had been completed. This was followed by a letter sent by Lieutenant Jewell from Gibraltar:

The Launching of the Body

Most Secret and Personal

From: The Commanding Officer, H.M. Submarine *Seraph*.

Date: 30th April, 1943.

To Director of Naval Intelligence.

Copy to F.O.S.

(for Lt.-Cdr. The Hon. E. E. S. Montagu, R.N.V.R.) personal.

Operation Mincemeat

Weather: The wind was variable altering between S.W. and S.E., force 2. It was expected that the sea breeze would spring up in the morning, close inshore, as it had on the previous morning in similar conditions.

Sea and swell—2:0—Sky overcast with very low clouds—visibility was patchy, 1 to 2 miles—Barometer 1016.

2. *Fishing Boats:* A large number of small fishing boats were working in the bay. The closest was left, about a mile off, and it is not thought that the submarine was observed by them.

3. *Operation:* The time of 0430 was chosen as being the nearest to Low Water Lisbon (0731), which would allow the submarine to be well clear by dawn. The canister was opened at 0415 and the body extracted. The blanket was opened up and the body examined. The brief case was found to be securely attached. . . . The "Mae West" was blown up very hard and no further air was needed. The body was placed in the water at 0430 in a position 148° Portil Pillar 1.3 miles approximately eight cables from the beach and started to drift inshore. This was aided by the wash of the screws going full speed astern. The rubber dinghy was placed in the water blown up and upside down about half a mile further south of this position. The sub-

105

marine then withdrew to seaward and the canister, filled
with water and containing the blanket, tapes and also the
rubber dinghy's container, was pushed over the side in position 36°37′30 North 07°18′00 West in 310 fathoms of water
by sounding machine. The container would not at first sub-
merge, but after being riddled by fire from Vickers gun and
also .455 revolver at very short range was seen to sink.
Signal reporting operation complete was passed at 0715.

A sample of the water close inshore is attached.

N. A. JEWELL,
Lieutenant-in-Command.

This letter included a description of the condition of
the body; there was rather more decomposition than
we had expected (perhaps due to oxygen trapped in
the clothing and blanket), but not more than was to be
expected had the body been floating half immersed in
the sea for some days.

Later on I got a more detailed account from a member of the ship's company—I got it at secondhand and,
as my go-between was a journalist by profession, the
picture that is conjured up by his account is much more
vivid than anything that I could record. I therefore
give it just as I received it:

As the *Seraph* slid from the shadow of her depot ship and
down the Clyde, the commander—he was only twenty-nine—
saluted from the conning tower, then went below.

Of the five officers and fifty ratings on board, only he
knew the secret of his odd piece of cargo.

106

The Launching of the Body

Wisecracks

The cylindrical metal canister now rested in a forward chamber of the submarine.

Because of its weight and shape, the six ratings who manoeuvred it into place joked about "John Brown's body." And there was many a wisecrack about "our new shipmate, Charlie."

To-day, ten years later, those fifty ex-members of the *Seraph's* crew will be shaken to learn how close to the truth they were.

They had been told in the briefing for the trip that the metal canister contained a secret weather-reporting device to be floated experimentally off the coast of Spain. It was actually marked "Handle with Care—Optical Instruments—for special F.O.S. shipment."

For ten days the *Seraph* sailed and her crew saw nothing of the sun. Surfacing only at night, she was off Huelva, on the south-west coast of Spain, undetected and according to schedule, on April 30.

The spot selected for floating "Major Martin" ashore was 1,600 yards off the mouth of the Huelva river.

In the afternoon the *Seraph* ventured an inshore reconnaissance. The periscope revealed a fishing fleet of about fifty vessels. But the prevailing mist and a mile detour helped the submarine to escape detection. Then she went back to the sea bed for the rest of the day.

Mysterious

Zero hour was 4.30 in the morning. When the *Seraph* surfaced again it was dark as pitch. The new moon had set and the ebb tide was just on the turn.

107

The Man Who Never Was

Through the conning tower went the five officers, and the submarine was trimmed down until an inch of the calm sea lapped over the casing. The mysterious canister was hauled aloft.

Only then, with all ratings below, did Lieutenant Jewell let his officers into the secret. Lieutenant Jewell told them that the canister at their feet contained a corpse. The operation, he said, was part of an Allied plan to deceive the enemy into drawing his defensive forces away from the spot selected for the main thrust of the Mediterranean invasion.

Phoney invasion plans were to be "planted" on the enemy through the medium of the body of this man purporting to be "Major Martin," victim of an air crash at sea.

Huelva had been chosen for the "plant" because it was known that the German agent there was being well fed with military intelligence by local collaborators.

What a story to be sprung on you suddenly in the middle of the night with the Atlantic lapping round your boots. But if the junior officers were shaken by their commander's dramatic and gruesome revelation, they did not betray it.

Only reaction was the comment from one of them: "Isn't it pretty unlucky carrying dead bodies around?"

Tension

Then quickly and quietly the five set about their task. While three kept watch, the other helped Lieutenant Jewell to unlock the bolts of the canister with the spanner attached to the case. Ten minutes they worked before the lid came away.

Then the blanketed body was slid gently from its vacuum coffin. For a moment the tension was relieved as the officers stiffened with silent respect in the presence of death.

108

The Launching of the Body

On his knees again, Lieutenant Jewell plucked at knotted tapes and the blanket fell away.

There followed the final check. Were the Major's uniform and badges intact? Was his hand gripping the handle of the all-important despatch case? Was the case securely strapped to his belt?

Everything in order, Jewel bent low to inflate the Major's "Mae West."

Only one thing remained—though it was not in the routine instructions. Four young officers bent bare heads in simple tribute as their commander murmured what prayers he could remember from the Burial Service.

For them, sworn to secrecy, these words from Psalm 39 held a special significance:

"I will keep my mouth as it were with a bridle: while the ungodly is in my sight. I held my tongue and spake nothing: I kept silence, yea, even from good words; but it was pain and grief to me."

A gentle push and the unknown warrior was drifting inshore with the tide on his last, momentous journey. "Major Martin" had gone to the war.

The risk that Lieutenant Jewell had taken in going so close to the shore had given us every possible chance of success. We could now only wait to see how Major Martin would carry out *his* part of the job.

10 Major Martin
Lands in Spain

ON THE 3rd MAY we received a signal from the Naval Attaché in Madrid. He had been informed by the Vice-Consul at Huelva that the body of a Major Martin, Royal Marines, had been picked up just off-shore by a fisherman on the 30th April. The body had been duly handed over to the Vice-Consul and had been given a full military funeral, at which the Spanish Services and civilian authorities were represented, at twelve noon on the following day in the cemetery at Huelva. There was no mention in the Attaché's message of the black official briefcase or of any official papers.

There then followed an exchange of signals between the Admiralty and the Naval Attaché. If the papers had been what they purported to be, it was obvious that, when the death of Major Martin and the arrival of his body in Spain became known at Combined Operations H.Q., there would have been a realisation of the fact that a most secret document had gone astray, and reference to Sir Archibald Nye would have re-

110

vealed the full measure of the disastrous "leak" of strategic information that might have taken place. In those circumstances, increasingly pressing messages would have been sent to the Naval Attaché, urging him to try to get the documents back at all costs, but warning him that he must take the utmost care not to show undue anxiety lest that should alert the Spaniards to the importance of the documents and encourage them to open or "lose" them. We naturally had to act as if the whole affair was genuine, and the signals were therefore on those lines.

We started by a signal on the 4th May stating that Major Martin had some papers with him which were of great secrecy and importance, and instructing the Attaché to make a formal demand for them. If they were not forthcoming, he should make very discreet but searching enquiries at Huelva to see if they had been washed ashore and, if so, what had happened to them. If he did recover them, he was to signal to "D.N.I.— Personal" the names of the addressees; he was not to open the envelopes, but to return them as quickly as possible to D.N.I.

We followed that by another signal informing him that it had been ascertained that there were three letters, of the utmost importance, and that they were believed to be in a black official briefcase with the Royal cypher on it. He was again warned on no account to arouse the interest of the Spaniards in the documents.

We learned from the Attaché, in reply to the first signal, that the Minister of Marine had informed him, in answer to a studiously routine enquiry, that the documents had been passed through "Naval channels" and would only reach Madrid via the Spanish Naval H.Q. at Cadiz. This would take some days. The Attaché had learned that the Vice-Consul at Huelva had had no opportunity to get the briefcase or other documents.

Then, on the 13th May, the Attaché informed us that the Spanish Chief of Naval Staff, in the absence of the Minister of Marine, who was away, had just given him all Major Martin's effects, including a black briefcase —the latter was open with a key in the lock. The Chief of Naval Staff had said that "everything was there," and the Naval Attaché had thanked him.

Although the Attaché had gained a strong impression that the Chief of Naval Staff knew at least something of the contents of the letters, he considered that there was no reason to think that that officer would divulge his knowledge to anyone. Of course, we did not suspect that officer of any breach of faith—but if *he* knew of the contents it would be certain that others would also know. Things were going well—the "leak" was starting.

Our optimism was strengthened by the next message

that we received from the Attaché. The Minister of Marine himself had referred to the papers when he saw the Attaché on Saturday, the 15th May. Apparently, he had heard, while in Valencia, that the papers had arrived in Madrid, and had immediately given orders to the Chief of Naval Staff to hand them over at once. He had done this lest someone might have had an unauthorised look at them, which might, he said, be a serious matter.

Nothing that had been said to the Minister of Marine before he left Madrid could have given rise to such anxiety about the documents, so we had no doubt at all that the envelopes must have been opened. That being the case, we were confident that there must be at any rate *one* Spaniard "in the know" who would pass the information on to the Germans. How close the co-operation was in fact we were not to learn until after the end of the war.

Meanwhile, discreet enquiries in Huelva filled in some of the details of what had happened. We learned with absolute certainty that a fisherman had noticed a floating object and had hailed a nearby launch, which took it on board. The object, which turned out to be the body of Major Martin, was landed on the nearest beach by the launch and handed over to an officer who happened to be exercising a detachment of infantry there.

A naval judicial officer was summoned, and he took

113

charge of all the documents and personal effects. The body, after identification, was removed to the mortuary at Huelva for medical examination by a doctor, who certified that the man had fallen into the sea while still alive and had no bruises, and that death was due to asphyxiation, through immersion in the sea since five to eight days before. An American Air Force pilot who had crashed into the sea on the 27th April was then asked to inspect the body in case he could identify it, but he (naturally) could not do so.

The man whom we knew to be the chief German agent in the vicinity had soon learnt of the landing of the body. He quickly ascertained the details, including the names of the addressees of the letters in the brief-case, and had tried to get copies of all the documents, but he was not successful owing to the chance fact that, as the military patrol had been present to take charge of the body, the naval judicial officer had been called in, and neither he nor his associates had the right kind of contact with that particular official.

Although we were confident that all had gone well, we wanted a final check, and we waited impatiently for the return of the documents that Major Martin had carried; eventually they reached London and were promptly submitted to scientific tests. Before sending them out, we had taken precautions, which I obviously cannot specify, which would help us to check whether the envelopes had been tampered with and, though the immersion in sea water made certainty impossible, we were now able to say with some degress of confidence from the physical evidence that the letters, or at least two of them, had been removed from the envelopes, although the seals appeared to be intact.

When we added this information to that which we had received from Huelva and from the Naval Attaché, we were quite satisfied. There was little doubt that the Spaniards had extracted the letters and knew what was in them, and that the German Intelligence Service knew of the important addressees; we could rely on the efficiency of the Germans to get all that they wanted out of that situation. We were sure that our confidence in the Spanish end of the German Intelligence Service would not be misplaced. It was now up to Berlin to play *its* part.

Meanwhile, we must say farewell to Major Martin. He had served his country well, and we felt that it was up to us to see that his last resting-place should be a fitting one and that proper tribute should be paid to him, even if all this had to be done under pseudonyms. We were glad to be able to show respect to him without any danger to the success of the operation in which he had played so vital a part. Indeed, by doing what our instinct required of us, we would make it more difficult for the Germans to check the Spanish doctor's verdict—a verdict with which we were entirely satisfied. Frequent visits to the grave by British officials and their representatives would at least deter any exhumation by the Germans or Spaniards before the tombstone could be laid.

First of all we got the Naval Attaché to arrange for a wreath to be placed on the grave from Pam and the family; next we arranged that a tombstone should be laid as soon as possible and, finally, I wrote to the Naval Attaché, asking him to thank the Vice-Consul at Huelva on behalf of Major Martin's family for all the trouble he had taken, and the consideration that had been shown, and asking also that photographs of the grave might be taken, as they would be treasured by the family and by Major Martin's fiancée, to whom he had so recently become engaged.

The wreath was composed of flowers from the garden of an English mining company at Huelva; the gravestone was of plain white marble and bore the inscription, "William Martin. Born 29th March, 1907. Died 24th April, 1943. Beloved son of John Glyndwyr Martin and the late Antonia Martin of Cardiff, Wales. *Dulce et decorum est pro patria mori.* R.I.P."

We could do no more for him, although we were deeply in his debt and felt that very soon many thousands of his fellow countrymen and their American allies might owe their lives to him as they landed on the shores of Sicily. Indeed, my confidence in that probability was shared by now by those in authority: I had sent a message to Lieutenant Jewell to let him know

116

Major Martin Lands in Spain

that his part of the operation had been completely
successful: as it was undesirable to send my message
by signal, in case it aroused talk, I decided that Lieutenant Jewell would know what I meant when I wrote,
"You will be pleased to learn that the Major is now
very comfortable" on an ordinary picture postcard.
But the Chiefs of Staff went one better; they sent a
message to the Prime Minister, who was by then in
Washington; it also had of necessity to be cryptic and
read:

"Mincemeat Swallowed Whole."

11 We Tidy Up in England

WE (and by this I mean all of us on the Allied side) had by now done our part of the job; if I may use a simile, we now had only to stone-wall, keeping our end up until close of play came with the landings in Sicily, leaving the Germans at the other end to do the scoring for us.

So, on the whole, we sat back and waited developments. However, as the days went by, we remembered that *The Times* used to reach Lisbon by air and the Germans might be keeping an eye on the casualty lists which were published from time to time. I therefore checked the average period that elapsed between a death and the subsequent announcement in the newspapers; it appeared as a general rule to be not more than about five weeks, and that, from the 24th April, would bring us to the first week of June.

Should we include Major Martin's name in such a list? Was it worth the complication involved? The landings in Sicily were planned for the second week in July, and the Germans could hardly be certain that the name of a genuine casualty would *have* to appear before then; and, if the deception had caused them to take any action, they would have done so before the first week of June and could hardly remedy any mistake —or even begin to do so—before we landed. On the other hand, it was always possible that the assault on Sicily might be delayed for some reason. After some hesitation, we decided that an omission to insert the name might do harm and that it was better to be sure than sorry.

Eventually, however, we were indeed sorry that we had added this embellishment to our creation, but fortunately only for the trouble that it gave us and not because it did any harm. As regards our objective of deception, all went smoothly and our phenomenal luck held. It was quite easy to get the Casualty Section of the Commissions and Warrants Branch of the Admiralty to accede to D.N.I.'s request that they should include the name of "Temporary Captain (Acting Major) William Martin, R.M." among the "Killed" in the next casualty list—I forget what explanation I gave when I conveyed the odd request. The announcement duly appeared in the issue of *The Times* dated Friday, the 4th June, 1943. We will probably never know whether the Germans did in fact spot this name, but, if they did, they would have found, in the same list, the names of Rear-Admiral P. J. Mack, D.S.O., and of Act-

The Man Who Never Was

ing Captain Sir T. L. Beevor, Bt., R.N. It had already been announced in the newspapers that these two officers, with others whose names had not been given, had died when an aeroplane had been lost at sea. What could be more plausible than that Major Martin had died with them—and the fact that it was that list which happened to be the next one was due to pure chance. It makes me hope that the Germans *did* spot that list, as it would be a pity if anything so artistic as that had been wasted.

But it was then that trouble started over here; casualty lists were studied by departments of whose existence I was blissfully unaware and by others whom I had forgotten. I was given a little experience of the sort of trouble which I would have had on a much larger scale had I allowed the messages passing between us and the Attaché in Madrid to have the normal distribution.

The Naval Wills Department wanted to know whether Major Martin had made a will—and if so, where was it? The Medical Director-General's Department wanted to know whether Major Martin had been killed in action, died of wounds, died on active service, or what, so that their statistics could be kept in order.

Fortunately, the precautions that I had taken to ensure that any enquiries about Major Martin (or any of his documents) were adequately dealt with worked satisfactorily. I heard of these enquiries at a sufficiently

120

early stage for me to be able to prevent their spreading too widely, but I had to deal with the departments concerned. I racked my brains what answer to give. I could not refer the Wills Department to McKenna & Co., the solicitors who had written to Major Martin about his will before he departed.

I had by now fully appreciated the truth of the aphorism, "Oh, what a tangled web we weave when first we practise to deceive," and was getting into the swing of it. I told the heads of each of those departments that they need not worry about Major Martin, or record him or his death. I explained that he was a special agent who had been sent on an important mission after having been given (with the First Sea Lord's authority) the cover of naval rank as an officer in the Royal Marines; after all, that account was perfectly true as far as it went. I only "forgot" to mention that he was already dead before any of that happened.

With D.N.I.'s authority, I impressed on them the vital need for secrecy, and they undertook to deal with the matter in their respective departments. The nearest we ever came to the operation "leaking" was over.

I might, perhaps, add that some years later, after I had been demobilised, people were still compiling other lists, and I suddenly got an urgent request to visit the Naval Intelligence Division. They had received other similar enquiries about Major Martin and wanted to know how I had dealt with such enquiries in the past, so that the same answer could be given again.

But apart from this matter of the casualty list, "Operation Mincemeat" was no longer in our hands. We had played our part and Lieutenant Jewell and Major Martin had played theirs. What were the Germans doing?

12 The German Intelligence Service Plays Its Part

THROUGH THE END OF MAY, through June and into July 1943 we had nothing on which to rely for our belief that we had succeeded in our plot, except for our faith in the thoroughness of the German penetration of Spain and the gullibility of the Germans. We were sure that we had succeeded in getting the documents to the Germans and that, now that we had achieved that first step, the picture presented to them was so complete and so authoritative that no Intelligence staff could fail to be certain that it had scored an epoch-making triumph.

We could picture the Intelligence chiefs rubbing their hands; they would be bound to preen themselves at the thought that the painstaking care and efficiency with which they had built up their organisation in Spain, and the liaison with important Spanish official-dom, which was Admiral Canaris's [1] special pride, had

[1] The Head of German Military Intelligence and Espionage.

at last proved its worth. In the past that organisation must have provided Berlin with much information about ship movements through the Straits of Gibraltar as well as intelligence gained in the British Isles and America and transmitted through Madrid, but that was to be expected of any such service. Besides, it had clearly been badly at fault before the assault on North Africa, when, so far as we could judge, the Germans had been taken by surprise. Now, at last, it had scored a real triumph.

To be able to provide the Operational Staff with an exact copy of a letter from a Vice-Chief of a General Staff to the Commander of an army in the field (and such a letter as this one) was beyond the wildest hopes of any experienced Intelligence officer—a fulfilment of the daydreams of his hopeful youth. Such information as the letter contained, if acted upon efficiently by the General Staff, might avert a disaster, or might result in the infliction of a crushing defeat on the Allies at a crucial moment in the war, and thus alter the whole history of the world.

It was for this reason that I had fought so hard against the suggestions that we should play safe, that we should use this plan to plant some minor misinformation contained in documents passing between officers of junior rank. If the letters that Major Martin had carried had been of that sort, not only might the Germans not have made the effort to get copies, but even if they had, they might not have relied on them when making strategic decisions. But what Sir Archibald Nye wrote to General Alexander *must* be true; the Vice-Chief of the Imperial General Staff must *know* what the Allied plans were—*he* could not be himself the victim of a "cover plan" or misinformed. If the German Intelligence Service swallowed these letters as genuine, they would have to "go to town" on them—and no General Staff which got such information with its Intelligence Service's *imprimatur* of genuineness could fail to base its strategy upon it.

So we sat back and waited. D-day of "Operation Husky" came, and the assault went well. Sicily is roughly a triangle standing on its point, and the Allies landed in the early hours of the morning of the 10th July on either side of this point and advanced rapidly up the sides of the triangle as well as across the middle. There were many elements that added to the surprise which was achieved, such as the rough weather and the "moon period" which was chosen, but that surprise certainly did nothing to shake the confidence of our group that we had succeeded with "Operation Mincemeat" and contributed our bit.

As Intelligence reports and documents gradually filtered in from Sicily, that view was confirmed; there seemed to be little doubt that the Germans had switched the effort that they had put into preparing the defences of Sicily, away from the south (where we

in fact landed) to the western angle of the triangle and
the northern side, which would have been the danger-
points if we had been making a diversionary assault
during an invasion of Sardinia, or an assault after
Sardinia had been captured. Not only were most of
the later minefields, demolitions and defences built in
the north of Sicily, but the total of defences and reinforcements in the island was less than had been expected and surprisingly deficient in the south and east.
On the information that was available, it was decided
officially that our part in the deception had been
successful. The view formed by those in authority on
the whole operation was summed up when Admiral
Cunningham reported, "The very efficient cover plan
and the deceptive routeing of convoys played their
part" in the surprise achieved—how preponderantly it
was due to the former we were only to know later.

For real knowledge of the extent and degree of our
success did not come until very much later—not, in fact,
until some months after "V.E.-Day."

I was quietly slogging away one morning in my stuffy
and ill-ventilated room in the bowels of the Admiralty
—winding up my work, writing records of what had
been done, for the guidance of those in future wars
who would never have time to read them (or think
them worth reading), and impatiently waiting for the
date for the demobilisation of my "Group" to come
round—when the telephone bell rang. It was D.D.N.I.,[1]

[1] Deputy Director of Naval Intelligence.

and his voice was so distorted with laughter that I found it hard to understand what he was saying, though I gathered that he wanted me in his room. So I went up there and, still shaking with laughter, he pushed some documents across the table to me. I picked them up and recognised them, in spite of the fact that the first words that caught my eye on the upper one were *"Lieber Grossadmiral"*! They were the "Mincemeat" letters, or at least the German translations of them, finishing their long journey!

D.D.N.I. then explained the cause of his laughter. An officer was in charge of the sorting and translation of the German naval archives which had been captured at Tambach in Germany. He had come up to D.D.N.I.'s room that morning with a very worried face, and had asked for instructions; his report was as follows:

In the file of documents that he was examining he had discovered "these two documents": one was a copy of a most secret letter from the V.C.I.G.S. to General Alexander and (he said) it looked as if there had been a fearful breach of security, as well as probable breaches of all sorts of regulations; normally, he ought to hand copies of letters of military importance over to his opposite number in the War Office, but this affair seemed to be so "hot" and fraught with high level complications that he felt that D.N.I. might like to handle it himself on his level!

D.D.N.I. had recognised the letters and put the officer's mind at rest. There then began a search for other documents bearing on the matter, and we soon found evidence of the completeness of our triumph over the German Intelligence Service.

As we had anticipated, they had immediately recognised the vital importance to their Operational Staff of these documents, if genuine, and had wasted no time.

Their agents in Madrid must have telegraphed the contents of the documents and an account of their discovery to Berlin early in the first week of May, because we have found reference in a later document to the fact that an Intelligence appreciation of Allied intentions had been circulated by signal on the 9th May before the "original documents" had been received in Berlin.

When the German Intelligence Service in Berlin received this information, they had obviously reacted as we expected them to do, and had demanded evidence to support the authenticity of the documents, for the first written report from Madrid had been followed by a second and more detailed one; this latter indicated that still further enquiries would be made. But time was short; Berlin had clearly appreciated the importance of the information and had decided that the details given by Madrid were convincing. And they had indeed, "gone to town" on it!

The first document of importance was an Intelligence appreciation which had been attached to a translation into German of the letter from Sir Archibald Nye to

The German Intelligence Service

General Alexander. It was dated the 14th May, 1943, and had been stamped with the "most secret" instructions: "To be circulated personally! Not through Registry!" The circulation marked on it was to the Commander-in-Chief of Naval Staff, Admiral Doenitz, and on the 15th May his Chief of Staff had initialled it and marked it with a cross, in blue pencil, to signify that Doenitz should read it himself; this the latter did, obliterating the cross in green pencil with his personal "squiggle" and the figures 18 to indicate the date when he read it on his return to his H.Q. from his visits to Mussolini and Hitler; there were also two other officers included in the circulation.

This document read as follows:

Subject: Captured Enemy Document on Mediterranean Operations.

Attached herewith are:

(*a*) Translation of the captured letter from the Imperial Staff to General ALEXANDER.

(*b*) Appreciation thereof by the (German) General Staff.

The contents of further captured documents are unimportant. Exhaustive examination by 3 Skl. revealed the following:

1. The genuineness of the captured documents is above suspicion. The suggestion that they have intentionally fallen into our hands—of which the probability is slight—and the question whether the enemy is aware of the capture of the documents by us or only of their loss at sea is being

129

followed up. It is possible that the enemy has no knowledge of the capture of the documents.

Against that it is certain that he knows that they did not reach their destination.

2. Whether the enemy will now alter his intended operations or will set an earlier date for their commencement must be taken into consideration, but seems unlikely.

3. *Probable Date of the Operation*

The matter is being treated as urgent; yet there is still time on the 23rd April to inform General Alexander by air courier of General Wilson's proposal to use Sicily as cover-target for the assault in the Eastern Mediterranean, wherein he is requested to reply immediately in the event of his supporting Wilson's opinion, "as we cannot postpone the matter much longer." In this case the Imperial General Staff considers altering the planning both in the Eastern and Western Mediterranean, for which there is still time.

4. *Sequence of the Operations.*

It is presumed that both operations will take place simultaneously, since Sicily is unsuitable as a cover-target simultaneously for both.

5. The Tobruk area comes into consideration as a starting-point for the operations in the Eastern Mediterranean. Alexandria is not considered, as in this case Sicily would have been absurd as a cover-target.

6. It is not clear whether the deception worked by the cover-target concerns only the period up to the beginning of the operations or whether in fact a cover-operation would be used as well as the actual assault.

7. It is *not* clear from the attached whether *only* the 5th and 56th Divisions will be landed in the Eastern Mediter-

ranean (at Araxos and Kalamata). However *only* these two Divisions are to be reinforced for their assault. It is always possible that all assault troops and targets are included with them.

8. It should be emphasized that it is obvious from this document that big preparations are in course in the Eastern Mediterranean as well. This is important, because considerably less intelligence about preparations has reached us from this area than from Algeria, owing to their geographical situation.

The first point that strikes one is that the German Intelligence Service is already committing itself to the categorical assertion that "The genuineness of the captured documents is above suspicion," and, although they do prudently cover themselves with a reservation that they are enquiring into the possibility of a "plant" and the extent of our knowledge of the fate of the documents, they are already saying that the possibility of the first "is slight." They have also already decided that we would be "unlikely" to change our plans or hasten the date of the assault; anyone with experience of the complexity and detail involved in the planning and launching of large-scale operations would agree with that view at least!

Another point which illustrates how, when one is working a deception of this kind, one has to put oneself into the mind of the enemy and to try to assume *his* degree of general knowledge is the statement in Para-

graph 5. The Germans say that Sicily is impossible as
a cover target for an operation by troops based on
Alexandria—presumably because they consider the
distance to be too great. Had it been *our* Staff who
read the document, the reaction would have been
different: they knew that the distance was not too great
and that troops from Alexandria could be used in an
assault on Sicily, as, in fact, took place.

I need not consider the rest of the document in detail,
as I will deal in the next chapter with the Operational
Staffs' appreciations of the documents. But this appreciation does reveal the care with which every word
and implication of the V.C.I.G.S.'s letter was studied.

This document was followed by another report
circulated by the German Intelligence Service which
was dated the 15th May, 1943. It read as follows:

Subject: *British Official Mail Washed Ashore Near Huelva*
    The following points were cleared up in a conversation
on 10.5.43 with the official concerned, a Spanish staff officer
with whom we have been in contact for many years:
    1. Clutched in the hand of the corpse was an ordinary
briefcase which contained the following documents:
    (*a*) A piece of ordinary white paper containing letters
        addressed to General Alexander and Admiral Cun-
        ningham. This white paper bore no writing on it.
        Each of the three letters was in a separate envelope
        with the usual form of address and directed person-

132

ally to the addressee, sealed apparently with the sender's private seal (signet ring).

The seals were in perfect condition. The letters themselves, which I have had in my hands in their re-sealed envelopes, are in good condition. For reproduction purposes the Spaniards had dried them with artificial heat and then placed them in salt water for twenty-four hours, without greatly altering their condition.

(b) Also in the briefcase were the proofs of the pamphlet on the operations of the Combined Operations Command mentioned by Mountbatten in his letter of the 22nd April, as well as the photographs mentioned therein.

The proofs were in perfect condition, but the photographs were quite ruined.

2. The messenger also carried a note-case in the breast pocket of his coat with personal papers, including his military papers with photographs (according to these, he was the Major Martin referred to in Mountbatten's letter of the 22nd April), a letter to Major Martin from his fiancée and one from his father, and a London night-club bill dated the 27th April.

Major Martin therefore left London on the morning of the 28th April, the same day that the aircraft came to grief near Huelva.

3. The British Consul was present at the discovery and is fully informed about it. The expected suggestions by the British Consul that the documents should be handed over to him were set aside under the pretext that all articles found on the body, including all papers, must be laid before the local Spanish magistrate.

The Man Who Never Was

After being reproduced, all documents were returned to their original condition by the Spanish General Staff and definitely give the impression—as I was able to see for myself—that they had not been opened. They will be returned to the English to-day through the Spanish Foreign Office.

Further enquiries are being made by the Spanish General Staff concerning the whereabouts of the pilot of the aircraft, who was presumably injured in the crash, and an interrogation of the latter about any other passengers.

From the point of view of our little group, this was a most fascinating document. It fully justified the care with which we had built up the personality of Major Martin, so that the very "reality" of that officer carried conviction as to the genuineness of the documents that he was carrying, although it does reveal how chance would render some details important and others unimportant. It also reveals how accurate we were in our belief, on which the whole operation was based, that the Germans would have complete access to anything that interested them, once it was placed in the hands of the Spanish Staff.

The first point that emerges is that, as I have already said, we need not have worried whether the attachment of the briefcase to Major Martin by a chain was plausible or not as the Germans were told that he had the briefcase clutched in his hand; so the inefficiency of the Spaniards, as well as their co-operation with the Germans, helped us.

I do not follow the reference in Paragraph 1 (*a*) to a

"piece of plain white paper" round the envelopes;
either this was something that some Spaniard put
round them to preserve them from stains or some paper
from the bundle of proofs of the Combined Operations
pamphlet had become misplaced; anyhow, we had not
wrapped up the envelopes. Also the seals were official
seals with the Royal Coat of Arms.

Then we noted that the personal papers in the wallet
had been extracted and inspected, and we were glad
that the letters from Pam and Major Martin's father
had not been missed—that artistic effort was not wasted!
Also Lord Louis Mountbatten's letter to Admiral
Cunningham is shown to have played its intended part
in establishing who Major Martin was.

But this report illustrates one of the greatest difficulties that has to be faced in carrying out a deception.
The deceiver can only supply his opponent with the
material and has to leave that opponent to draw the
deductions from it: for that reason he has to gauge
both the efficiency and the intelligence with which his
material will be treated. I feel that our deduction as
to the intelligence of the Germans was about right, but
we may have put their efficiency too high, for they
made two extremely careless mistakes—both about
dates.

As can be seen by a comparison of the photographs
of Lord Louis Mountbatten's letter to Admiral Cunningham and the photostat of the German translation
of the same document (between pages 64 and 65), the

Germans were too careless to copy the date correctly. The letter was dated 21st April, but the Germans, either in copying the letter or in translating it into German, altered the date to the 22nd April.

As it happened, that did not matter, but the other mistake was much more dangerous. There is a reference in the report to "a London night-club bill dated the 27th April"; we came to the conclusion that that must be based on a careless reading of the stubs of the theatre tickets. The invitation to the Cabaret Club was not only not a bill, but it was not dated at all. It could not have been the bill dated the 24th April for his room for several nights at the Naval and Military Club, since that did not look like a night-club bill, and surely even the Spaniards would not have mistaken the "In and Out" for a night-club! So we came to the conclusion that this error was due to a careless confusion between the stubs from the Prince of Wales' Theatre and the invitation to the Cabaret Club. That did not matter, but the mistake in the date might have been more serious.

The report decided, as we intended the Germans to believe, that Major Martin flew from England the day after he had had his farewell party; but the error in the date fixed that departure as having taken place "on the morning of the 28th April, the same day that the aircraft came to grief near Huelva." Had the Germans considered the opinion of the Spanish doctor, of which

136

The German Intelligence Service

at least their agent in Huelva must have been aware, as to the date of death, and linked it with this date of departure, they might have become suspicious. The Spanish doctor had, not unreasonably, put the date as several days before the body was recovered on the 30th April: the shortest time that was suggested was some five days. So, on that basis, the aircraft disaster which caused Major Martin's death must have taken place on about the 25th April.

I am not sufficient of a philosopher to work out what can be deduced from this. It could be argued that we had been lucky that no one noticed this discrepancy and that our deception ought to have been "blown." I hope it is not too egotistical to say that I do not accept that. We had provided the Spaniards and Germans with all the clues from which they could draw the deductions that we wanted. While I suppose it would be absurd to say that we were entitled to reasonably competent and intelligent co-operation from the other side, I think we can say that we *had* provided the right clues and that they *did* draw the right deductions, even if those deductions were only reached by a cancelling out of compensating errors!

Anyhow, the report shows that the Germans did deduce that Major Martin *must* have travelled by air and that the disaster to the aircraft took place on a date consistent both with his departure and his state when he arrived.

The Man Who Never Was

The next paragraph of the report also interested us. It revealed that our view of the efficiency of German-Spanish co-operation at Huelva was fully justified. It recorded how, when the fortuitous intervention by a military unit and a naval judicial officer precluded immediate access to the documents, the efforts of the British Vice-Consul to take charge of them were "set aside" under a "pretext." We knew that we could "trust" the Spaniards!

Finally, there is the record of the fact that the envelopes, with the letters restored to them, and other papers were not returned until after the German agent had himself inspected and handled them. That he thought that the letters "gave the impression that they had not been opened" does not surprise me: they would have given me the same impression if we had not taken precautions.

So, as far as the German Intelligence Service was concerned, we had won; as far as they were concerned, one could repeat the view of the Chiefs of Staff, as regards the Spaniards, "Mincemeat Swallowed Whole." The Intelligence Service, at any rate, had accepted the whole thing as genuine. But, as I have indicated before, that would have been only a hollow victory if the German Operational Staff had failed to take the same view and had continued to go all out in preparing to meet an invasion of Sicily. But they swallowed it also, and they also "went to town."

138

13 The German High Command Gets Busy

THE INFORMATION that we gleaned from the German naval archives captured at Tambach was equally revealing with regard to the reactions that "Operation Mincemeat" produced from the German High Command. The results that we gained were far beyond our wildest hopes.

Our guess as to what the Germans originally thought the Allies were going to do after Tunisia had fallen had been right, and we had even under-estimated the difficulties that we were up against. We found a copy of a message sent by the German High Command to their army in Tunisia in February of 1943. They had decided that our next operation would be in the Mediterranean, and that it would be against one of the large islands; they put the order of probability as Sicily first, with Crete second and Sardinia and Corsica following behind. So, when we were doing our planning in London we were right in thinking that, from a very early stage, the Germans would put Sicily at the head of the betting, and as our preparations grew in the western Mediterranean they would have realised that *those* could not be for an assault on Crete, with an un-reduced Sicily barring the way. We had guessed right about that, but the message included the statement "from reports coming in about Anglo-American landing intentions it is apparent that the enemy is practising deception on a large scale." They were going to turn out to be accurate about that also, but had the Chiefs of Staff known how alert the Germans were for deception, I wonder whether we ever *would* have got permission to launch "Mincemeat"!

The documents reveal that this strategic appreciation was maintained right up to the beginning of May, 1943. And then, on the 9th May, the whole picture changed: the news of the capture of Major Martin's documents had reached the High Command.

On the 9th May an Intelligence appreciation must have reached the High Command, for we found the following document in the file just after the appreciation dated the 14th May mentioned in the last chapter:

Further to my 2144/43 dated 9.5.43, following appreciation has been made on receipt of original material:

1. A landing in the eastern and western Mediterranean on a fairly large scale is anticipated.

(*a*) Target of the operation in eastern Mediterranean under General Wilson is the coast near Kalamata and the stretch of coast south of Cape Araxos (both on the West coast of the Peloponnese). The reinforced 56th Infantry Division is detailed for the landing at Kalamata and the reinforced 5th Infantry Division at Cape Araxos. It is not known whether both divisions will land in force or in part only. In the first instance, a lapse of at least 2–3 weeks would be required as the 56th Division on 9.5.43 was engaged at Enfidaville with two brigades and must first be rested and embarked. This solution, which embraces a certain delay before the landing can take place, appears to be the more probable from the way in which the letter is written. However, if the landing is to be effected by only certain units of both divisions, it could be made at any time, as one brigade of the 56th Division and 1–2 brigades of the 5th Division are probably already available in the actual starting-area (Egypt-Libya). Code-name for the landing on the Peloponnese is "HUSKY." The Anglo-American General Staff has proposed a simultaneous cover operation against the Dodecanese to General Wilson. Wilson's decision thereon was not yet taken on 23.4.43.

(b) Target for the operation under General Alexander in the western Mediterranean is not mentioned. A joking reference in the letter points to Sardinia. Code-name for this operation is "BRIMSTONE." The proposed cover target for operation "BRIMSTONE" is Sicily.

2. Maintenance of completest secrecy over this discovery and utmost limitation of circulation of this information is essential.

On a point of detail, this document gave me great pleasure. I had already congratulated myself that the German agent in Madrid had bothered to send on a copy of the seemingly unimportant letter from Lord

Louis Mountbatten to Admiral Cunningham, unlike his treatment of the equally unimportant letter to General Eisenhower. *Was* it because of the hint that we thought we had failed at Dieppe? But Paragraph 1 (*b*) of this appreciation showed that my heavy-footed joke about sardines had gone home—"a joking reference in the letter points to Sardinia"; it was not the same letter, but that can be excused in an appreciation of this kind. The German sense of humour is a great asset.

The German Intelligence Service had swallowed the deception: now the High Command accepted this view. It may well be that we have Hitler to thank for this, for we know, from the diary of Admiral Doenitz's conferences with the Fuehrer, that by the 14th May Hitler was convinced of the genuineness of the documents, and what they foretold. For Doenitz had been sent to Italy to try to stiffen Mussolini after the North African disasters, and he reported to Hitler on his way back to his own headquarters before he himself had seen the documents; in reply to a question by Hitler as to Mussolini's views on "Anglo-American intentions," he reported that the Duce was convinced that we would attack Sicily; and here is his record of Hitler's reply:

The Fuehrer does not agree with the Duce that the most likely invasion point is Sicily. Furthermore, he believes that the discovered Anglo-Saxon order confirms the assumption that the planned attack will be directed mainly against Sardinia and the Peloponnesus.

It is clear that Hitler was completely sold on the idea that we were intending to land in Greece and, now that he had come to this conclusion, he stuck firmly to it. So much so that, on the 23rd July, nearly a fortnight after the Allied landing in Sicily, Hitler *still* believed that the main operation was going to be an invasion of Greece, and appointed his favourite general, General Rommel, to command the forces that were being assembled there. On the 25th July Rommel flew to Greece, whence he had to be hurriedly recalled to take over the command in Italy and rally the defence of that country after the fall of Mussolini.

But it would be unfair to put too much blame on Hitler. On the very same day that Hitler had corrected the Duce's opinion, the 14th May, the Official War Diary of the German Naval High Command recorded the fact that the General Staff of the Army had come to the definite conclusion that the documents were genuine; they concluded that the assault would be on Sardinia, but that there might be a diversionary attack on Sicily.

So, by the 14th May, 1943, the Operational Staffs, the Supreme Command and the Fuehrer himself were all convinced. "Operation Mincemeat" was completely successful. It remained for us to discover just what this eventually meant to the "Anglo-American" forces.

I do not know in any detail what the German Army and the Luftwaffe were doing, but that they were doing something considerable is evidenced by an order sending the 1st German Panzer Division all the way across Europe from France to establish its headquarters at Tripolis, a town in the Peloponnesus ideally situated to command resistance against landings which included Kalamata and Araxos. When one considers the enormous effort involved in a journey of this kind for a complete Panzer Division, and how it put that force "out of the war" for the time being, one might say that that alone would have far more than repaid the effort that we put into "Operation Mincemeat," even if we had not assisted the invasion of Sicily at all.

We also found in the German records a memorandum of the fact that the German Foreign Office had been asked to warn the Turkish Government that troops and shipping were being moved to Greece, but to stress that there were no hostile intentions against Turkey.

This precaution was not surprising when we consider the extent of the German preparations, for, although, as I have said, I have no details of the Army and Luftwaffe movements and activities, they may well have been large if we judge by the German naval activity, of which we naturally found a much more detailed picture among these documents.

By the 20th May the Naval High Command had

144

ordered [1] the laying or the completion of three new German minefields off Greece, including one off Kalamata itself. The German Admiral commanding in the Ægean was ordered to take over control of minefields that the Italians were laying off the western coast of Greece, and German coastal-defence batteries were to be set up in territory under Italian control. These were only some of the steps that were "envisaged or have already been taken" by that date as the Germans had appreciated that almost the whole coast of Greece, as well as the Greek islands, was threatened, though it was hoped that the Allied assaults might be beaten off in spite of German weakness in that area.

These instructions were completed by orders to establish R-boat [2] bases, command stations, naval sea patrol services and other safeguards: the effort to be put in was intense.

The dividend from "Mincemeat" was growing, and that it was a dividend from "Mincemeat" alone is established by documents which show that these orders were based on Major Martin's letters (a point that would have to be concealed in the operational orders themselves for reasons of security). Another indication is given by the statement in the orders that the likelihood of a large scale Allied landing in the eastern as well as the western Mediterranean had been established in

[1] See Appendix I.
[2] German Motor Torpedo Boats.

spite of the fact that "so far indications of the preparation of large numbers of landing craft have reached us only from the western Mediterranean"; in addition, it is possible for those who compare both documents— the "Mincemeat" letter and these orders—to trace the connection.

Shortly after this, in early June, a whole group of German R-boats was sent *from* Sicily *to* the Ægean! Our dividend was indeed growing fast.

Meanwhile, things were moving in the western Mediterranean area also. I can summarise the main reaction best by reference to an order sent out on the 14th June in Hitler's name by General Keitel, Commander-in-Chief of the Supreme Command of the German Armed Forces. These orders [1] are clearly based on the German appreciation that the use of Sicily as a "cover target" for the assault on Sardinia might involve a diversionary attack on that island (they took a similar view of our use of the Dodecanese as a cover target for the eastern Mediterranean operation: see Appendix I and the appreciation of the 14th May). The operation of that factor on the mind of the German Staff is evidenced also by the location of the German defensive measures which we found in Sicily, as I have already recorded.

We also found a record of the fact that a strong Panzer force with its ancillaries and supplies for two months was sent to Corsica in June by an order issued

[1] Appendix II.

146

in Hitler's name, and from now on there was a growing emphasis on the reinforcement of Sardinia and Corsica, with the north coast of Sicily coming next in priority.

On the 9th July, *the day before we landed in Sicily,* Keitel sent out a long appreciation which he says is that of Doenitz. This appreciation covered not only both the eastern and western Mediterranean, but also future Allied strategy based on operations in both those areas; in it he concludes that an attack on all three islands, Corsica, Sardinia and Sicily (either all together or one at a time), as well as the Greek operation, is possible. Doenitz estimates that there are enough Allied troops in the whole of North Africa to provide for both operations and then to exploit the bridgehead that the Allies may be able to form in Greece; his appreciation is that a major landing on the coast of Italy (after the capture of the Italian islands) is unlikely, as the Germans could react fast in Italy, whereas in Greece their reinforcements and supplies would necessarily be slow, and from Greece the Allies could attack the Roumanian oilfields, and the political effect of such an operation on Hungary, as well as Roumania, might be great. Finally, Doenitz's conclusion, promulgated by Keitel, is that "the western assault forces appear to be ready for an immediate attack," which could begin at any time (how right he was!), whereas "the eastern force appears still to be forming up" (how wrong he was: they in fact took part in the invasion of Sicily).

147

The Man Who Never Was

On the early morning of the 10th July our forces had landed in Sicily, but the Germans still could not believe that that was the real assault (and that the documents must have been a plant): the German High Command asked that a special look-out should be kept by the German agents on the shores of the Straits of Gibraltar for convoys which would be going to attack Corsica and Sardinia—they presumably still thought that the landings in Sicily (although on the side of the island that they did not anticipate) were a diversion to draw attention from the main operation.

But by the 12th July even the German belief in the accuracy of the "Mincemeat" documents had begun to weaken—after all, the invasion of Sicily was obviously genuine and had been going on for two days.

We found two messages passing between the German Naval Commander-in-Chief in Italy and the Naval High Command. In the first, the Commander-in-Chief complains bitterly that the departure of the 1st R-boat Group (which had been sent to the Ægean for the defence of Greece) had prejudiced the defence of Sicily, as a gap had been left in the patrols, which were consequently ineffective. He stated that the shortage of small craft was "chronic" and that the departure of any more boats, as ordered, would have a serious effect both on defensive work and on escort work. The reply stated that reconnaissance reports had shown the Allies to have engaged so much in Sicily that there was little probability of landings in Greece until the Sicilian operation was over; the defence of Greece could take second place "for the time being" (was "Mincemeat" *still* having some influence on the High Command as well as on Hitler?), and the order for seven boats of the 11th R-boat Flotilla to go to the Ægean was cancelled: these boats could remain under the orders of the Commander-in-Chief, Italy.

So the immediate repercussions of "Operation Mincemeat" had finally ended—except, for the German forces still sitting idle in Greece. The survey that has been made of its results can be summarised as follows:

As regards the working out of the "Operation": we fooled those of the Spaniards who assisted the Germans; we fooled the German Intelligence Service both in Spain and in Berlin; we fooled the German Operational Staff and Supreme Command; we fooled Keitel; and, finally, we fooled Hitler himself, and kept him fooled right up to the end of July.

As regards the eastern Mediterranean: we caused immense effort to be put into the defence of Greece, with the creation of minefields, shore batteries, etc.; we caused a concentration of troops in Greece which justified the appointment by Hitler of Rommel to command them; these troops included a Panzer Division which had to be sent right across Europe; all this was completely wasted effort from the German point of

149

view and diminished the potential defence of Sicily and of Italy.

As regards the western Mediterranean: we caused an increase in the fortification and reinforcement of Corsica and Sardinia at the expense of that of Sicily; we caused the defensive preparations in Sicily to be largely diverted from those coasts of the island where the Allies in fact landed to the coasts where they did not land; we caused the Germans to send R-boats away from Sicily to the Ægean, thus opening a gap in their defences which "prejudiced the defence of Sicily" as well as creating a shortage of escort vessels.

All this can be traced from the contemporary documents, and I think that I can fairly claim that our dividends from the "Operation" were indeed enormous—far greater than we had anticipated in even our most sanguine moments. It is for others to assess how many British and American lives were saved by "The Man Who Never Was" during the conquest of Sicily, and what effect his exploit had on the course of the war.

Envoi

RATHER THAN CONCLUDE on a somewhat bombastic note —a note that I feel to be owed to the memory of the man who really was, and who became "Major Martin, Royal Marines"—I would like to add something that puts my own part in the "Operation" into its proper perspective.

As the result of what we already knew of the success of "Operation Mincemeat," I was awarded the Military O.B.E. in 1944. When he was pinning the medal on to my uniform jacket, His Majesty asked me where it was that I had earned it, and on my replying, "At the Admiralty, Sir," I could see his eyebrows go up in some astonishment. He followed with another question: "What did you get it for?" Taken by surprise, I could only ejaculate: "Part of the planning of 'Operation Husky,' Sir."

That reply of mine made me realise how the entire thing fitted together and, as I have said, put the whole picture into its proper perspective. "Operation Mincemeat," with all its thrill and "glamour," was just an integral part of the planning of a modern operation.

151

Appendix I

Copy of 1st Naval War Staff 1 Ops. 1942/43, Most Secret, S.O. only, of May 20.43

From a teleprinted signal (outgoing) to:

Supreme Command of the Armed Forces/Operations Staff of the Armed Forces.

Copy to: Naval Group Command South, C.-in-C. G.A.F., Operations Staff of the G.A.F. 1a (Naval), Captain Mossel, Supreme Command of the Army/Army General Staff Naval Liaison Officer, Captain Weygoldt.

Cleared as Single Address Message.

Most Secret for S.O. only.

The Naval War Staff has examined exhaustively the possibilities of enemy landing operation in the South-Eastern Area and has come to the following conclusions:

(1) (i) The possibility of enemy landings in the Eastern as well as the Western Mediterranean must be reckoned with although reliable evidence about the preparation of a large number of landing craft is so far available from the W. Med. only.

152

(ii) Possible starting-points for landing operations:

(*a*) ARTA-PYRGOS area: Gulf of Arta, Gulf of Patras, the coast South of Cape Araxos and on both sides of Pyrgos and also islands off these areas, especially Corfu and Cephalonia.

(*b*) The South coast of the Peloponnese: Navarino, Gulf of Corone (Kalamata) and Gulf of Marathon.

(*c*) CRETE: Preferably the North coast, on the South coast Mesara Bay and Hierapetra, but only with limited forces.

(*d*) RHODES.

(*e*) Islands in the ÆGEAN: Leros, Milos, Chios, Mytilene and Lemnos.

(*f*) The East coast of the PELOPONNESE and Central GREECE: Gulf of Nauplia, Gulf of Petali (East coast of Attica).

(*g*) SALONICA: Gulf of Salonica, Gulf of Orphani.

(*h*) THRACE: Gulf of Cavalla and the coast to the East of Thasos.

(iii) It can be assumed that the enemy will probably make an initial landing where he believes there will be the least resistance and where he expects the greatest results in the shortest time. Therefore an initial landing on CRETE can be ruled out for the moment; in view of the advanced state of the development and equipment of the Fortress of CRETE a very considerable expenditure of strength would be required and a pre-

requisite would be subsidiary operations to obtain airfields in the Dodecanese and Peloponnese close to the
scene of operations. Further, the capture of CRETE
would only represent a partial accomplishment of his
aims. A thrust past CRETE into the ÆGEAN, the occupa-
tion of the most important islands and a landing attempt on the East coast of the PELOPONNESE and
Central GREECE is likewise improbable. An attempt at
an immediate thrust into the area of SALONICA and
THRACE need not be reckoned with. For such operations the enemy would require very large forces to protect his supply-routes. Considerable losses would be
unavoidable as long as German air and light Naval
forces (S-boats) can be operated from CRETE.

(iv) In the opinion of the Naval War Staff landing
attempts are most likely to be made in the Greek West
coast area where the CORFU-ARTA-PYRGOS region offers
the greatest prospects of success.

Possibilities: a thrust from the North towards
LARISSA-VOLOS, cutting off Central GREECE with the
PELOPONNESE; in the centre an advance towards Central GREECE and ATTICA. In the South a drive for the
CORINTH Isthmus. The islands off this coast (especially CORFU and CEPHALONIA) would become very valu-
able bases in enemy hands. Special attention is drawn
to the exceptional importance of these islands.

Simultaneous subsidiary landings are probable at
NAVARINO (a good harbour for Naval forces operating

for the protection of landings and supplies), KALAMATA (airfield) and perhaps also the Gulf of MARATHON. A subsidiary thrust through TRIPOLIS to CORINTH. Simultaneously or shortly beforehand a diversionary operation against the DODECANESE (RHODES) is to be expected.

(2) The defensive power of the areas in the greatest danger is still weak. Nevertheless in the opinion of the Naval War Staff it should be possible to throw back attempted enemy landings if he attacks with only limited forces. According to evidence from the Army General Staff available to Naval War Staff the enemy has at present only a few divisions available in the E. Med. Also the available transport space is sufficient for these forces only.

All measures must therefore be taken to reinforce rapidly the defensive strength of the areas which are specially threatened. The construction of a secondary line of defence in the rear (roughly in the N. GREECE-SALONICA area) is only to be considered when the other has been accomplished.

(3) The following immediate steps are envisaged or have already been taken by the Naval War Staff:

(i) Laying of German minefields: off KALAMATA in the process of completion, CERIGO Strait complete, CERIGOTTO Strait in preparation. Group Command South (Admiral Ægean) to exert his influence for the laying of mines by the Italians on the West coast of GREECE.

(ii) The installation of coastal batteries, also in the

155

Italian-occupied area (the decision of the Supreme Commander of the Armed Forces has been requested).

(iii) PIRÆUS and SALONICA are intended as the principal bases for Naval forces and are or will be appropriately supplied. MELOS, LEROS and LEMNOS as auxiliary bases will receive only limited supplies for Naval forces.

(iv) The possibility of installing operational bases for S-boats on the PELOPONNESE and CRETE is being explored.

(v) Preliminary discussion with C.-and-C. G.A.F. South East concerning reconnaissance and offensive action by the G.A.F. after the approach of enemy operations has been established (air attacks on the landing fleet where possible while it is still in its port of departure and mining these harbours from the air).

(vi) Preparation of a patrol-service with coastal defence vessels to the West, South and East of CRETE.

(vii) Preparation of a Command Station for Admiral Ægean at SALONICA to ensure uninterrupted control in the event of it proving necessary to move the headquarters.

Naval War Staff Reg. No. 1st Naval War Staff 1 Op. 1492/43. Most Secret. S.O. only.

Appendix II

Reg. No. Naval War Staff 1 17 189/43. Most Secret.

Distribution: Copy No.1. Chief Naval War Staff
                2. Naval War Staff
                3. 1a
                4. 1 ops
                5. 1 m
                6. Naval War Staff qu A
                7.   ”   ”   ”   ”   ”
                8. 1 f
                9. 1 b
                File 13.

Teleprint MBBZ 02175 of 14.6.43 23.34.

Most immediate GWASL 02633 14.6 2130.

To Supreme Command of the Navy, Naval War Staff.

Also for: General Staff of the Army, Inspector-General of Armoured Troops, Supreme Command of the Navy (Naval War Staff, C.-in-C. South, Home Staff, Overseas Branch).

MOST SECRET

(A) The FUEHRER has issued the following orders for the reinforcement of SARDINIA and SICILY.

The Man Who Never Was

(1) Measures to be taken by the Army General Staff:

(i) Every island to be provided with a Fortress Infantry Regiment to the strength of one regimental staff with an H.Q. Coy. and 4 battalions.—3 March Battalions of the June draft to ITALY may be used if necessary. In this connection the FUEHRER stressed especially the need to be strongly equipped with local weapons suitable for defence against armour and land attack. For this purpose recourse can even be had to French 2.5 and 3.7 centimetre anti-tank guns with stick grenades.

The regiments must be ready to move by 28.6.43. If it is not possible to procure the anti-tank guns needed for SICILY by this time the remaining anti-tank guns must be sent on by 20.7 at the latest.

(ii) SARDINIA to be provided with a Fortress Artillery Abteilung for costal defence.

Equipment—2 batteries of 17-cm. guns.

1 battery of 10-cm. guns

(The latter are available from C.-in-C. South.)

To be prepared to depart as soon as possible.

(iii) The SARDINIA detachment to be provided with 1 anti-tank coy. with 12 anti-tank guns for each regiment.

Every lorried infantry coy. of the SICILY detachment to be equipped with 2 anti-tank guns. If heavy and medium anti-tank guns are not at first available, recourse must be had to light anti-tank guns firing stick grenades. The anti-tank coys. should however be equipped with heavy and medium anti-tank guns.

(iv) The SARDINIA Armoured Coy. to be expanded to an armoured Abteilung with at least 50 tanks (of which at least 25 will be Mark IV) by supplying the necessary units and weapons. To be prepared to move off as soon as possible.

(v) The setting up of an armoured coy. of 20 tanks Mark IV for the 215th Armoured Abteilung in SICILY. (This coy. to be transferred to compensate for the Tiger coy. which was handed over to the Hermann Goering Division.) To be prepared to move off by 15.7.43.

(vi) Several W/T detachments to reinforce the Signals Coy. of the SARDINIA Command.

(2) The Supreme Command of the Navy is to form a coastal artillery Abteilung from 3 newly-commissioned batteries and is to transfer them to C.-in-C. South for despatch to SICILY on call.

(3) C.-in-C. South's other requirements must be given lower priority unless a special order to the contrary is given.

(B) (1) The Army General Staff will report to the Supreme Command of the Allied Forces/Operations Staff of the Armed Forces:

(i) The proposed equipment of the Fortess Regiments with anti-tank guns (statement of calibre) and other heavy weapons (including rifle-grenade apparatus).

(ii) Details of the distribution of the anti-tank guns according to calibre amongst the other newly-created units and reinforcements required.

(iii) The times at which the individual reinforcements will be ready to move off (to be reported also to Home Staff [Overseas Branch]).

(2) The Supreme Command of the Armed Forces will report to Operations Staff of the Armed Forces and Home Staff (Overseas Branch) when the costal artillery Abteilungen are ready to move off.

(3) Home Staff (Overseas Branch) will be responsible for the rapid passage of these reinforcements.

(*Signed*) KEITEL,
Supreme Command of Armed Forces/
Operations Staff of the Armed Forces.
Op. No. 002820. Most Secret.